Birth Equality:

How a Child Called Grace Taught Me the Value of a Human Life

Nick Park

Evangelical Alliance
IRELAND

Birth Equality:
How a Child Called Grace Taught Me the Value of a Human Life

Printed in Ireland by SPRINT-print Ltd

Cover design by Jonny Lindsay
Photograph of Grace Park by Fiona Storer

Published by Success Services Ireland on behalf of
Evangelical Alliance Ireland
22/24 Foley Street, Dublin 1
Ireland

www.evangelical.ie

ABOUT THE AUTHOR

Nick Park grew up in Belfast, Northern Ireland. His family were Quakers, and viewed themselves as being on neither side of the Protestant/Catholic divide. This was not always an advantage, and Nick subsequently experienced sectarian violence from both factions.

An atheist by conviction, Nick was part of the burgeoning Belfast punk rock scene celebrated in the movie *Good Vibrations*. His involvement with heavy drinking and drug abuse resulted in alcoholism and homelessness.

He experienced a dramatic religious conversion in 1981, which set him on a different course. He has served for many years as a church minister, first in the Salvation Army and then in Pentecostal churches. Despite some popular misconceptions of evangelical ministers living lavish lifestyles, the reality is usually much more humble. At various times Nick has supplemented his income by working as a security guard, a painter and decorator, a hotel porter, a care assistant in a retirement home, an industrial cleaner, a warehouse operative, a taxi driver, a newspaper distributor, an insurance salesman, a community newspaper editor, an author, a publisher and a bookseller.

Today Nick is Pastor of the Solid Rock Church in Drogheda, Bishop of the Church of God denomination in Ireland and Executive Director of Evangelical Alliance Ireland. His wife, Janice, is a gifted musician and songwriter who is also a qualified coach driver. Indeed, if you have ever parked your car in one of the Long Term Car Parks at Dublin Airport, or taken a bus from

Dublin Airport to Belfast, then you may have been one of her passengers!

Nick and Janice Park live with an Old English Sheepdog in Dromin village in County Louth. They have one adult daughter, Kirsty.

Nick travels extensively, speaking at conferences around the world. He is a frequent contributor to newspapers and magazines. He has also authored a number of books, including his autobiography 'From Touching Rock Bottom to Touching the Nations,' all of which are available through Amazon or at www.nickpark.ie

CONTENTS

INTRODUCTION

Why would I bother writing this book? More to the point, why should you bother reading a book on a pressing social issue written by a Christian leader?

Tony Campolo, the American sociologist and Baptist pastor who prayed the benediction at the 2016 U.S. Democratic Convention after Hillary Clinton was nominated as the party's Presidential candidate, has said, "Mixing religion and politics is like mixing ice cream and manure. It doesn't do much to the manure but it sure does ruin the ice cream."[1]

You don't have to look too far to find examples of religious meddling that, while failing to make any appreciable positive change in our societies, have certainly damaged the reputation and effectiveness of the Church. At other times, religions have caused great harm and hurt by trying to enforce their dogma upon others. Some of the greatest atrocities in history have been committed by religious believers. Of course the religious have no monopoly on intolerance and cruelty – the last century has amply demonstrated that those who deny the existence of God have an equal capacity for totalitarian bigotry and suppression of independent speech and thought.

I describe myself as a 'Christian Secularist.' By that, I mean that I advocate a complete separation of Church and State, with religion being accorded no special privileges by society, and also being subjected to no special restrictions or discrimination. The ideal society, in my view, is one that is officially religiously neutral – with the followers of all religions, and those who follow no religion at

1

all, having a level playing field upon which they are free to live according to their consciences, free to express their opinions, and can tolerate and respect those who believe differently.

One very reasonable conclusion to be drawn from such an approach is that religious dogma should not be the basis for governing society or for framing laws. If the best argument anyone can present for proposed civil legislation is 'because my holy book says so' then they would be better off keeping quiet.

So does this mean that people of faith should have no voice or platform at all when we discuss complex ethical issues or contemplate changing our Constitution or laws? By no means. Silencing a large section of the population because they happen to be religious would be a betrayal of the principles of secular democracy. Such censorship would be anything but a level playing field.

Also, democratic societies do give publicity and prominence to statements and opinions from organisations that represent a considerable number of citizens. Like it or not, a massive number of people in our society still practise a religious faith. It might not be as dominant as it once was, but more people in Ireland will attend a religious service each weekend than the combined totals of those who either play or watch GAA, soccer or rugby.

Each time I hear someone confidently asserting that religion and politics should be kept separate, my response is to ask, 'So would you prefer it if slavery hadn't been abolished after all?' I might equally ask whether we would prefer to live in a society where children as young as thirteen were legally trafficked for the purposes of prostitution. Or I could ask if the United States should reinstate racial segregation.

The reason why slavery is no longer legal, why a realistic age of consent protects children from sexual abuse, and why racial segregation was outlawed, is because Christian believers, motivated by their religious beliefs, fought against injustice, cruelty and discrimination. But they didn't achieve these reforms by lecturing others that they should obey the Bible. They made alliances with unbelievers by presenting clear and compelling reasons why a kinder, fairer and more inclusive society was necessary.

Furthermore, social reformers such as William Wilberforce and Martin Luther King didn't impose dogma from a position of judicial and cultural power. Instead, they spoke from the margins of society. They identified with the wounded and the voiceless (if you would like to read a fuller account of these historical campaigns then you can order my little book 'The Gospel and Human Rights' from www.nickpark.ie).

This book stands within that honourable tradition of religious activism. It is consistent with a consistent broadening and more generous application of human rights, often achieved despite vocal opposition from those who, against history, would limit, narrow and diminish the application of those same human rights.

I speak as a representative of a small religious minority in Ireland. I have no political clout, and I wouldn't want to impose my religious views on others even if I had the power to do so. But I am deeply concerned when a well-orchestrated media campaign seeks to violate the human rights of those who are least able to defend themselves. I am also moved to indignation when organisations that we have traditionally looked to as defenders of human rights inexplicably seek to deny the application of those rights to all human beings.

There's another reason why I wrote this book, and why you should read it. Everyone loves a good story. Christians, just as much as anyone else, face challenges and tragedies. Our faith might often help us to cope in those situations, but our doubts and fears are just as real as anyone else's. In the following pages you will read about a real-life family coping with a situation which, while thankfully rare, could still happen to any of us.

This book is not attempting to convert anyone to Christianity, nor is it trying to tell anyone else to follow Christian dogma. It doesn't ram Bible verses down anyone's throat.

What this book does attempt to do is to tell a deeply personal and difficult, but ultimately rewarding story. It also applies lessons learned from that experience to an ongoing national debate. In the end, no system of ethics or morality, religious or otherwise, counts for very much if it doesn't relate to the struggles of ordinary people like ourselves. But if more of us share our stories, and use those stories to encourage a fairer and more compassionate society, then the struggles can at least serve a useful purpose.

Nick Park
Executive Director, Evangelical Alliance Ireland
Easter Sunday, 2017

1

A CHILD SHALL TEACH THEM

The Calm Before the Storm

Before August 1989 I thought I already fully appreciated the value of a human life. My own life had seen a remarkable turnaround – breaking free from a destructive downward spiral of alcoholism and homelessness. I had experienced several brushes with death, including a brutal sectarian beating and a terrifying motorcycle accident, all of which caused me to appreciate waking up alive every new morning. I had met the most wonderful woman I could imagine, and watched her walk down the aisle on our wedding day, followed by the joyous joining of our lives and futures together. I had held my firstborn child in my arms, and, right there in the hospital maternity unit, had realised with startling clarity that here was another human being for whom I would quite willingly lay down my life if necessary.

So, yes, I thought I appreciated the value of a human life as much as, if not more than, anyone else. But that was before Grace Park came into our lives. We were living and working in the Northwest of England, and had a beautiful baby daughter, Kirsty. My wife, Janice, and I were eagerly anticipating the arrival of our second child. We did all the stuff that expectant couples do. I would rest my hand on Janice's belly and feel the baby kick. We would wonder if the little person in her womb was a boy or a girl. Would they grow up to play football for Ireland? Would they inherit Janice's musical gifts? Would they share my love of books and history?

I just used the word 'person' in respect to our unborn child. We always spoke of that child as a person. I don't think we ever uttered the word 'foetus' during the entire eight months of the pregnancy. We would have laughed out loud if anyone had ever tried to convince us that it was actually just a 'clump of cells' that was keeping Janice awake with those little kicks. No, like almost all expectant parents, we instinctively knew that what Janice was carrying inside her was a human life. It was a dependent life, certainly, and a vulnerable life. But to us that just meant that it deserved more care and attention.

That Moment When Everything Changes

A few months into the pregnancy, Janice had a routine ante-natal scan. This is supposed to be a moment of joyous anticipation, with smiling parents holding hands and gazing in awestruck wonder at the images on the ultrasound screen. Our scan didn't turn out like that. Instead we received the news that there were major problems. The baby's head looked far too small, and there wasn't enough fluid surrounding it in the amniotic sac.

Sometimes we experience gradual changes in life, and then sometimes there are sudden events that change your life irrevocably. That ante-natal scan was an instant doorway into another universe. We left behind forever the familiar world of new parenthood, routine baby clinics with jolly community nurses, warming bottles for night-time feeds and smiling mother and toddler clubs. Instead we found ourselves dumped into a bewildering world of incubators, grim-faced consultants, needles, blood-stained dressings, and machines that beeped and flashed as they dispensed fluids drop by drop.

Several years ago the relative of a family friend was killed by a falling tree during a fierce storm in the west of Ireland. My friend commented, "The poor boy must have been the unluckiest chap in Ireland. That area is so desolate and mountainous that you could drive for miles without seeing a tree. When he saw that tree coming down on him he must have felt as if life itself was fed up with him!"

Learning that your unborn baby is seriously ill is a bit like that. Of course you know that a certain percentage of parents will face such news, but you never expect it to happen to you. Those kind of things always happen to somebody else – don't they? What disturbed us even more was that there was no clear diagnosis. If we could have put a name on our child's condition, then at least we could have found out more about it. We would have been able to unearth some heart-warming inspiring stories of hope triumphing over adversity. But all we knew was that our baby was fighting for life before it had even had a chance to be born, and nobody could tell us how or why.

Two Lives

After that initial scan, everything moved at breakneck pace. A further scan listened to mother's and baby's heartbeats. I could hear Janice's heart beating firmly and loudly, albeit faster than normal due to her anxiety. You had to listen more carefully to discern the second heartbeat. It was fainter, more hesitant, but it was there! We were hearing the heartbeat of our baby. Of course that heart had been beating for months, unheard by anyone else, inside the womb. But hearing it for the first time brought home to us how this was an individual person, totally dependent on its mother, and yet already having a separate heartbeat and its own identity. We were in the middle of a medical crisis – and those two sets of heartbeats made us acutely aware that, whatever happened next, two lives were at stake.

Was it my imagination, or was that smaller set of heartbeats growing weaker? I looked at Janice, and I could see that she was thinking the same thing. She asked the nurse, "Is it supposed to sound like that?" The nurse, after listening more intently, ran to fetch a doctor. The doctor confirmed that the baby's heartbeat was slowing down. He announced, "Your baby is dying. We're going to have to act quickly if we're going to save it. We'll have to carry out an emergency Caesarean section."

Not imagining that this was on the cards, Janice had eaten a meal only a short time ago. Since she hadn't fasted the required period before an operation, she had to sign a disclaimer absolving the hospital from any responsibility if she choked and died during the operation. How different this was from the birth of our first child, Kirsty, almost exactly a year earlier. On that occasion I had been present in the delivery room, holding Janice's hand and making what I hoped were suitably sympathetic noises. But now I was pacing up and down outside an operating theatre – my mind racing with all kinds of possible dire scenarios.

When Grace was born she weighed just two pounds and thirteen ounces (1.28 kg). That's less than half the normal birth weight for a healthy baby. There was no holding our baby in our arms for that wonderful moment of bonding – she was rushed straight to the Special Care Unit and placed in an incubator. Later that evening, once I knew that Janice was going to be OK and had checked that she was sleeping peacefully, I went into the Special Care Unit. Grace looked impossibly small. How could anyone that tiny possibly survive outside of the womb? I pressed the palm of my hand against the transparent plastic of the incubator and willed her to keep fighting for life. She was wearing nothing except a tiny disposable nappy, and her painfully skinny chest was pulling in little shallow breaths from the oxygen that was piped into the incubator. Everything about this scene seemed so wrong. She should be wrapped in a blanket, lying in her mother's arms as we posed for celebratory photographs. There was no celebration to be found in watching her struggle for life in a transparent plastic box with no-one allowed to touch or hold her.

Over the next few days, Grace's condition gradually improved, and we were eventually able to hold and cuddle her. She was even strong enough to be removed from the incubator and placed in a cot instead. But there were obviously serious problems. She was unable to swallow milk or any other liquid. Every time she tried to feed, the liquid would 'go down the wrong way' causing coughing and choking. This, in turn, kept causing breathing difficulties and lung infections. The only ways the medical team could get nutrition into her body were through a drip, or by inserting a tube through her nose and directly into her stomach.

How Much is One Human Life Worth?

I remember one evening in particular. I was sitting beside Grace's cot, listening to her wheezing breath as she slept fitfully. I noticed how many medical staff were coming in and attending to her. I looked at the array of machines that were monitoring her vital signs. I tried to read the chart at the end of her cot, wondering what on earth the many different medications were supposed to be doing. Suddenly I thought, "This must be costing thousands!" I tried to calculate the cost of all the resources that were being funnelled into keeping Grace alive. We had no private medical insurance, so no-one was ever going to present us with a bill, but I estimated that her medical expenses for just one week probably amounted to more than I was earning in a year! At that moment I was profoundly grateful to be living in a nation that would provide our child with such care for free. I also reflected on the fact that, if Grace had been born in many other countries in the world, she wouldn't even have lived long enough to make it through the first day of her life. I asked myself, "How much is one human life worth?"

Years ago, when I worked in the financial services sector, I remember a successful businessman explaining the value of things. He pointed out that it was pointless having an estate agent to put a value on your house unless you could actually find someone who was willing to pay that amount. Without a purchaser, the house had no real value at all.

The British National Health Service was prepared to spend a huge amount of money to keep Grace alive, and that's how it should be. We would be outraged if babies were left untended to die because somebody somewhere wanted to save money. Why? Because we recognise that even the youngest and smallest human life has an immeasurable value.

That led me to ponder on what I would pay to save Grace's life. I knew immediately that I would willingly mortgage or sell everything we possessed if it could enable her to live. That is the value of a human life. I also realised that I would willingly lay down my life, if necessary, for this tiny baby that seemed determined to cling to life against all the odds. As a father, her life was worth more to me than my own life. That is the value of a human life. Furthermore, this estimation of the worth of Grace's life didn't suddenly pop into being at the moment of her caesarean delivery. It extended back to when I had felt her little feet kicking against Janice's belly, and when I had heard her little heartbeat slowing down inside the womb. Grace was only a week or two old, but already she was teaching me an important lesson about the value of a human life.

The strange thing is that, while I was thinking this through, I was sitting in a hospital that was the largest provider of abortions in that region of the country. Both before and after the moment of her birth, everyone had spared no effort to save Grace's life. Yet in another part of the same hospital, medical staff were using their training and expertise to end the lives of unborn children, many of whom did not suffer from anything like the undiagnosed condition which was making Grace so ill. So what did that say about the value of their lives?

Was my businessman friend right when he said that nothing held any real value unless someone was willing to pay for it? Could that possibly apply to human lives as well? Is another human being's life only of value if they are loved and wanted? Or is there something special about a human life that gives it an objective value, irrespective of whether anyone cares for it or not?

Some might see these questions as being religiously motivated, and it's true that I am a Christian believer. But, for me, these questions go far beyond religious dogma or one's personal beliefs about the existence of God. The inherent value of a human life is what inspires and informs the whole field of human rights, and that is an area of concern common to religious believers and to atheists or agnostics.

The basic concept behind all human rights law, including major international treaties, is that a human life has an objective worth that is not derived from whether they are valued by others or not. Martin Luther King taught us that if someone is despised by others, perhaps because of their race, gender or sexual orientation, that does not lessen their value. They still deserve to be treated with dignity, simply because they are human beings. In other words, you might be the most popular person in the world, but that does not give you any additional human rights over and above someone who is unloved and unwanted.

I had no doubt that Grace's life was indeed worth all the time, effort and money that was being expended on her care. I don't believe that I was overvaluing her life. And I could see no distinction between the concern and care that was devoted to her survival before her birth and after her birth. It wasn't as if she had no inherent value as a person the moment before her birth and then suddenly became precious and valuable the moment after her birth. Such a crude, almost magical, distinction seems more dogmatic and illogical than the claims of any religious sect.

If Grace's life was so important and valuable, both before birth and after birth, then on what grounds could anyone say that the lives of unborn children that were unloved and unwanted were not equally valuable? This self-evident truth led me to a conviction that has never left me. All human life is precious. And every child should have an equal right to be born.

That's why I maintain that it took the laboured breathing of a desperately sick and underweight baby to teach me the value of a human life.

2

A WRONGFUL LIFE?

Searching for a Diagnosis

A diagnosis can be bad news or good news. But at least, with a diagnosis, you know what you're dealing with. With Grace, everybody could tell that something was seriously wrong, but nobody could tell us exactly what. It was like an episode of the TV series *House*.

Different doctors would run batteries of tests, trying to pin a name onto Grace's condition. But each of these attempts would ultimately run into a dead end. Janice and I lost count of the number of times we sat in front of a consultant doctor's desk, listening to him explaining their progress. "Well," he would say, "We noticed that some of Grace's symptoms were indicative of …" – and we would hold our breaths nervously as he named some dreadful disease. Then he would continue, "… but if that was the case then the next test wouldn't have given us the results it did, so we can strike that one off our list." And, at that, Janice and I would exhale again.

Grace's symptoms were numerous. Some of them just seemed strange, whereas others had serious consequences. Her body appeared to lack the ability to react to temperature changes. For most of us, our bodies automatically help us out if we are too hot or too cold. When we get too hot, millions of glands release moisture as sweat. This moisture evaporates, and cools us down.

If we get too cold, our skeletal muscles automatically begin to shake, making us shiver. This movement creates energy as heat. For Grace, these automatic responses were all mixed up. She might get too cold, but, even though her skin was cold to touch, she would be soaked with sweat.

Grace appeared not to feel pain like other babies. She would cry, certainly, but this crying often seemed to be born out of frustration when she was constricted by medical equipment, rather than the physical pain of injections or treatments. Even when she did cry, she couldn't produce tears. Throughout her life, we never got to see a single tear roll down our daughter's cheek.

She remained far too small for a child of her age, and frequently vomited. Her muscle tone was poor, and her blood pressure fluctuated wildly. But the most serious symptom concerned her inability to feed normally.

When Food Becomes an Ordeal

Human bodies, when they work well, are really quite amazing. The process of swallowing food, which seems so simple and natural to us, is actually pretty complicated. As you eat or drink, your tongue pushes your food to the back of your throat, where there are two openings. The first opening is your oesophagus. This is where the food needs to go in order to make its way down to your stomach. The oesophagus is sealed off at top and bottom by two circular muscles, or sphincters, that prevent digestive acids from coming up into your mouth and make it possible for you to bend over without the contents of your stomach travelling in the wrong direction!

The other opening is your trachea, or windpipe, that connects to your lungs. When you breathe, the windpipe carries air from your mouth and nose down into your lungs. When you speak, the windpipe carries air back from your lungs into your larynx, or voice box.

As your tongue pushes your food to the back of your throat, a carefully coordinated process occurs that happens without you even being aware of it. Your voice box rises to block off your windpipe. This is why it's almost impossible to talk while swallowing, and probably why parents tell their children not to talk and eat at the same time! At the same time the sphincter at the top of your oesophagus automatically opens to receive your food, triggering peristalsis - a series of muscle contractions and relaxations that push the food down towards your stomach. Simultaneously, as a further protective measure, a little flap of cartilage behind the root of your tongue closes over your windpipe to seal it off from the food.

We've probably all had the unpleasant experience of laughing or coughing just at the moment of swallowing a bite of food. Even a tiny amount of food getting into the windpipe makes us choke, gasp for air, and even lose our voices. It can leave us feeling painful and uncomfortable for a considerable period of time.

The problem for Grace was that none of this automatic process seemed to work correctly. When she tried to swallow, the food would get into her wind pipe and make its way into her lungs. This was highly traumatic, provoking choking and vomiting. Then she would develop lung infections and pneumonia.

Janice and I had to learn to feed Grace via a tube. This meant wrapping her tightly in a sheet, so her arms were pinned to her sides. Even the smallest of babies will instinctively try to grab and remove a tube that is being forcibly inserted into their throat!

Then the tube had to be threaded down the back of her throat and into the oesophagus. This could take several attempts to get right, with the tube tending to slip into the wind pipe instead. As you can imagine, Grace would be retching and choking at this point.

Once the tube had been pushed all the way down into the stomach, we had to double check it wasn't in the lungs. This meant using a syringe to suck some gastric juices up the tube, and test them with litmus paper to ensure they were acidic. Then, using a much larger syringe, a nutritional liquid had to be poured down the tube. Forcing the liquid too quickly would cause it to back up in the oesophagus, and even to overflow into the wind pipe, so we had to hold the syringe up in the air for ten or fifteen minutes and let it slowly drain down.

The whole procedure took between twenty and thirty minutes. Grace would often be screeching the whole time, and Janice and I were frequently in tears by the time a feed was complete.

Even with all these precautions, there were many occasions when Grace would vomit some of her food back into her mouth, then, in attempting to swallow it again, it would drain into her lungs. So all of our best efforts still could not prevent our daughter's frequent bouts of pneumonia.

We didn't realise it at the time, but this tube feeding, which had to be repeated every four hours, would be the routine around which our lives were to revolve for the next four and a half years. This would be particularly tiring for Janice, as she would frequently be caring for Grace and Kirsty alone while I was at work.

The Diagnosis

Finally, we received a diagnosis. It was no wonder that it had taken the medical team months to reach this point. The consultant explained that Grace was suffering from an extremely rare condition called Familial Dysautonomia (FD), or Riley-Day Syndrome. FD is a progressive neurogenetic disorder which is found almost exclusively among Ashkenazi Jews. According to our consultant, there were only 25 recorded cases in history of non-Jewish FD patients. Since neither Janice or I are Jewish, there were obviously now 26 cases. There is no cure for FD, and most children with the condition die before their fifteenth birthday.

The autonomic nervous system is that part of our nervous system that controls our bodies without conscious effort on our part. Our breathing, the beating of our hearts, the swallowing of food, crying tears, blushing, shivering or sweating – these are all functions of the autonomic nervous system. If it doesn't work properly then normal life becomes impossible.

Despite her many physical problems, Grace was obviously a bright little girl. Already caring for one lively little toddler, we now had to adjust to the prospect of looking after a second child whose life would most likely be fairly short and who was going to need round-the-clock care and attention.

The 'Wrongful Birth' Case

Recently, the same rare condition from which our daughter suffered made headlines in the legal world.

Larry Sernovitz is a rabbi from Cherry Hill, New Jersey. In 2008, his wife, Becky, gave birth to a son, Sammy, with Familial Dysautonomia. Because she was an Ashkenazi Jew, and since over 3% of Ashkenazis are carriers of FD, she was screened to see if she herself was a carrier. But her doctor did not tell her that the test results were positive for FD. The Sernovitzes subsequently sued the Holy Redeemer Hospital in Philadelphia, arguing that if they had known that Becky was a carrier then they would have aborted their unborn child.

Obviously such a case has troubling moral and ethical implications. Many people feel deeply uncomfortable when parents appear to be saying that they wish their son had never been born. One major issue in the case revolved around the massive medical costs involved in caring for Sammy. If Larry and Becky Sernovitz won their case, then the hospital's insurers would foot the bills. If they lost, then the bills would have to be covered by Pennsylvania's taxpayers.

Pennsylvania had a law on the statute books forbidding such 'wrongful birth' suits. This was overturned by a Superior Court, but then the Pennsylvania Supreme Court ruled that the State law was valid and so the Sernovitz case could not proceed.

In a few States and countries, such legal cases are permitted. But most jurisdictions prohibit them, seeing the very idea that anyone's life is less valuable than anyone else's as a form of discrimination. In Germany, for example, wrongful birth suits would violate the Constitution which guarantees dignity of life to all.

A number of American organisations which represent the disabled, including the National Disability Rights Network, the Autistic Self Advocacy Network, and the National Down Syndrome Society, have argued strongly that the whole idea of 'wrongful birth' devalues and stigmatises people with disabilities as being unworthy of life.

Birth Equality

The diagnosis we received of Grace's condition certainly warned us that her life was going to be much more difficult than that of most children, but that did not reduce the value of her life by even a fraction. As far as we were concerned, Grace's life was just as valuable as everyone else's life, and she had an equal right to be born and to live. The physical challenges she faced simply meant that we, as parents, had an added responsibility to care for her. If anyone had suggested that her disabilities should somehow remove her right to life, then we would have been outraged.

The idea that a physical or mental disability should deny an unborn child the right to be born is not uncommon. Many countries routinely include a test for conditions such as Down Syndrome as part of their ante-natal procedures. When these tests prove positive, then the disabled child is usually aborted.

Future generations may well look back on this practice in the same way that we would look back today at historical practices that were previously seen as quite normal, such as slavery, torture, segregation, the binding of children's feet in China, or the burning of suspected witches. How, they might ask, could these people deny basic human rights to others in such a barbaric and systematic way?

The whole concept of human rights is based around one simple premise – that there is something unique about human beings. Most of us, whether we are religious or not, instinctively recognise that it would be fundamentally wrong and unjust to treat any category of people as if they were just animals. This sentiment is summed up in the famous words of the American Declaration of Independence, "We hold these Truths to be self-evident, that all Men are created equal, that they are endowed by their Creator with certain unalienable Rights, that among these are Life, Liberty, and the Pursuit of Happiness."

But is this truth, that all human beings have an unalienable right to life, really self-evident? History would suggest otherwise. Down through the years, human rights, including the right to life, have often been denied to entire categories of people.

3

THE BROADENING RIVER OF HUMAN RIGHTS

A Depressing Past

If we look back through the centuries of human history, we don't have to search too far to find examples of man's inhumanity to man. On every continent, we find records of people treating other people, not just as if they were animals, but worse than anyone would ever treat an animal.

This brutal disregard of other people's rights can be found among all races, among people of all religious persuasions and those with no religious belief, and among both the uneducated and the educated. Possessing a high intelligence, or grappling with the problems of philosophy, doesn't necessarily make a person more decent or compassionate. For example, Aristotle was a famous Greek philosopher from the fourth century BC who wrote one of the most famous ancient treatises on ethics – yet he argued that certain races of men were so inferior as to be fitted for nothing better than slavery.[2]

Some religions made fine-sounding declarations about the value of human life – such as the Judeo-Christian idea that humans possess an inherent dignity because they are made in the image of God. Yet the followers of these same religions often proved

21

themselves capable of committing the most appalling cruelties both among themselves and against others.

For most of history the idea that we are all entitled to be treated with dignity, and that we all possess certain rights simply on the grounds that we are human beings, was unknown or ignored. If those who were the victims of torture or injustice had even thought of protesting that their human rights were being infringed, they would have been laughed to scorn.

The Birth of Human Rights
(Well, for White Europeans)

The Enlightenment thinkers of the seventeenth and eighteenth centuries are often credited with coming up with our modern concept of human rights. Certainly, the likes of Locke, Voltaire, Hume and Kant were able to wax lyrical about 'the rights of man.' But if we explore their writings we soon discover that these rights didn't actually extend to black Africans.

John Locke (1632-1704) famously wrote that the law of nature obliged all human beings not to harm "the life, the liberty, health, limb, or goods of another."[3] Yet this same man was responsible for inserting in the Constitution of Carolina a clause that stated, "Every freeman of Carolina shall have absolute power and authority over his negro slaves, of what opinion or religion soever."[4]

Voltaire (1694-1778) is remembered as a champion of human rights and free speech. Indeed, an Australian human rights organisation, Liberty Victoria, annually presents a 'Voltaire Award' for those who promote free speech. So how did Voltaire use his free speech on behalf of African slaves?

It is a serious question among them whether the Africans are descended from monkeys or whether the monkeys come from them. Our wise men have said that man was created in the image of God. Now here is a lovely image of the Divine Maker: a flat and black nose with little or hardly any intelligence. A time will doubtless come when these animals will know how to cultivate the land well, beautify their houses and gardens, and know the paths of the stars: one needs time for everything.[5]

Another key Enlightenment thinker was David Hume (1711-1776). But his views on race were no more enlightened than those of Locke or Voltaire.

I am apt to suspect the Negroes, and in general all other species of men to be naturally inferior to the whites. There never was any civilized nation of any other complection than white, nor even any individual eminent in action or speculation.[6]

Immanuel Kant (1724-1804) is often remembered for his noble appeals to natural justice. For example, "Every man is to be respected as an absolute end in himself; and it is a crime against the dignity that belongs to him as a human being, to use him as a mere means for some external purpose."[7] Yet Kant also believed that Africans were incapable of education, except to be trained as slaves, and, although capable of being disciplined and cultivated, could never be civilised.[8]

You might wonder how someone like Kant could maintain two such contradictory positions. How could he speak so eloquently about the dignity and rights of men, but then deny those rights and dignity to men of another race? The answer is that Kant did not believe that every human being was a person in their own right. He maintained that what made you a person, and therefore worthy of respect and possessing certain rights, was the ability to reason and to make moral choices.

Today, you find echoes of this among certain proponents of abortion who insist that because an unborn child cannot make decisions or exercise choices, and because that unborn child is totally dependent upon its mother, then the unborn child does not qualify as a human being.

This is why, in debates about abortion, the unborn child is often referred to as a *foetus*, a *clump of cells* – or even as a *parasite*. If you can pretend that an unborn child is not a human being, then you don't have to worry about whether you are abusing their rights. One huge problem with this dehumanising language is that it doesn't just rob unborn children of their status of being persons and human beings - you can also use Kant's philosophy to similarly dehumanise young infants, people suffering from Alzheimer's disease, or those with profound mental disabilities. Since these categories of people aren't able to reason or make decisions, does that justify treating them as being less than human? And if the unborn child's inability to survive outside of the womb makes it a parasite, then surely the same would apply to conjoined twins? If one child cannot survive without being attached to his twin, does that make him less than human?

The whole point of human rights is that they protect the weak and the vulnerable from being exploited and abused by the powerful. Dehumanising the weak and the vulnerable, so as to deny their equal status as human beings, removes their protection and makes a mockery of the entire concept of human rights.

By artificially limiting those whom he recognised as being human beings and persons, Kant managed to talk a good talk about human rights, while simultaneously denying human rights to people of other races whom he suspected (quite wrongly of course) of being inferior to white Europeans.

Human Rights Broadened to All Races

Thankfully, the development of human rights thinking did not depend on these 'Enlightenment' thinkers. A British member of parliament, William Wilberforce, teamed up with a pottery manufacturer by the name of Josiah Wedgewood. They campaigned long and hard against slavery. They hit upon a wonderfully simple and yet effective idea, one that has been copied by almost every political campaign since – they invented the campaign logo!

Even though Wilberforce and Wedgewood were deeply religious, their logo was not a Bible verse. They wanted to appeal to principles of justice and fairness which would speak to both the religious and the non-religious. Their logo was a brooch that depicted an African slave kneeling in chains and accompanied by the words "Am I not a man and a brother?"

This appeal to our common humanity made more sense to the public than all of the Enlightenment thinkers' philosophical attempts to justify racism, or their sophisticated arguments to narrow or limit human rights to only some people. Of course it took a long campaign before slavery was abolished, because those who would limit human rights usually do so by appealing to our own fears and feelings of self-interest. It was frequently argued that, if Wilberforce and Wedgewood had their way in abolishing slavery, the economy would collapse. But that image of the kneeling African slave was just too powerful, and laws were passed that outlawed slavery.

In the United States, a similar process occurred, but there the most significant figure in the abolitionist movement was not a clergyman, a politician or a pillar of the business community. Harriet Beecher Stowe, the wife of a Bible College professor, wrote a novel that succeeded in leading the reader to imagine themselves in the shoes of a runaway slave. *Uncle Tom's Cabin* became a sensational best-seller, and millions of white Americans, irrespective of their religious beliefs, came to realise that African-Americans were people like themselves and deserving of the same dignity and respect.

Sadly, the combined forces of fear and self-interest can be a constant temptation and a hindrance to progress. Over a century after the publication of *Uncle Tom's Cabin*, another deeply religious campaigner in North America had to wage a bitter campaign, losing his life in the process, in the pursuit of a dream that white and black children could play together as equals who deserved equal dignity and equal rights. Martin Luther King's struggle against racial segregation was designated as a 'civil rights' campaign – but today we recognise that it was fundamentally a human rights struggle, demanding that African-Americans should not be treated as if they were less than human.

Today, thanks to these brave campaigners, we have a broader and more generous concept of human rights that cannot be limited by artificial barriers of race and ethnicity.

Human Rights Broadened to All Ages from Birth

Many societies throughout history have practised infanticide, or the killing of young children. Ancient Greeks and Romans used to leave unwanted children exposed on hillsides to die from cold, starvation, or to be consumed by wild animals.[9] In China, unwanted babies were drowned in a bucket of water known as 'baby water.'[10] In Japan, infanticide was known as *mabiki* – a horticultural term used to denote the uprooting of plants from an overcrowded garden.[11]

Sometimes this infanticide was because children were disabled or had a birth defect – even something as minor as a cleft palate. Often it was because the new-born child was a girl. Indeed, around the world thousands of new-born girls are still killed by their parents every year, a shocking practice that was exposed in the 2012 documentary film, *It's a Girl: The Three Deadliest Words in the World.*

Apart from infanticide, the abuse of children's human rights has been all too common for centuries. Frequently, as with most trafficking of children for sexual exploitation, and with female genital mutilation, this violence is also gender based. One major problem was that children were viewed as potential people in the making, rather than as human beings in their own right. Children were also deemed to be the property of their parents.

In the mid-nineteenth century there was remarkably little protection for children, even in the most industrialised and developed nations of the world. Children were exploited for cheap, or even slave, labour. At least in theory, if not in practice, legislation protected very young infants from sexual abuse – but it was common for older children to be trafficked for the purposes of prostitution. In Britain, the age of consent was thirteen.[12] In other countries it was even lower. In the American State of Delaware the age of consent was seven years old.[13] Adults could legally commit sexual acts against these older children, but the children themselves were not deemed to have control over their own destinies. They were, in effect, non-persons who could be pimped out without fear of prosecution.

Unsurprisingly, those in power did little to alleviate this situation. Human rights were not viewed as applying to children.

In Britain, the Salvation Army teamed up with a crusading newspaper editor called W.T Stead. Stead, who edited *The Pall Mall Gazette*, is often commemorated as being the first tabloid journalist. They formed a coalition of reformers, including clergy and prominent socialists. Stead wrote lurid articles which laid bare the seedy underbelly of Victorian London. These were considered so scandalous that stationers refused to stock *The Pall Mall Gazette*, and Stead had to recruit volunteers to sell the paper on the streets.

The counter-attacks against Stead and the Salvation Army concentrated on two issues. One was that they were discussing sexual matters, and thus offending against public decency. Apparently the existence of child prostitution was not as obscene as pointing out that the practice was occurring! The second objection raised against the reformers was that the scenarios they were describing were beyond belief. Children it was claimed, could not be bought and sold for the purposes of prostitution in the capital of the British Empire.

Stead, together with Bramwell Booth, the Chief of Staff of the Salvation Army, staged an innovative publicity stunt to demonstrate that such practices were indeed possible. They bought a fifteen-year-old girl for £5 – an incident that would later provide the inspiration for George Bernard Shaw's play, *Pygmalion*, and the film adaptation, *My Fair Lady*.

The girl, Eliza Armstrong from Lisson Grove, was being purchased, as far as her mother understood, for the purposes of prostitution. *The Pall Mall Gazette* publicised the transaction and a staged re-enactment of a common procedure for trafficking young girls.

Incredibly, the authorities reacted by prosecuting Booth and Stead. In the end, the case hinged on whether the girl's mother, rather than the father, had the right to sell her! Booth was acquitted, but Stead was imprisoned.

However, the publicity that accompanied the case caused such a public outrage that legislation was enacted to raise the age of consent to sixteen. This prompted other nations around the world to follow suit. The concept of human rights was broadened to include children as human beings in their own right, and hundreds of thousands of children were lifted out of legal sexual slavery.

A Clear Progression

As well as these landmark cases that we have mentioned, there has continued to be a steady broadening of human rights. Major international treaties have emphasised that human rights apply to all races, to women and children, to migrants and refugees, to religious minorities, and to those with differing sexual orientations. Some of these advances were prompted by people of faith. Others were won despite the opposition of religious institutions.

What is clear, is that the historical trend has been for human rights to be broadened and interpreted in ever more generous ways so as to embrace more and more people. It is also clear that those who oppose this trend have appealed to fear and self-interest in order to artificially limit the application of human rights.

Today, there are two overlapping categories in particular that are excluded by those who would artificially narrow and limit the extent of human rights. They are the disabled, and the unborn child.

Abortion is frequently used as a discriminatory tool. In many Asian countries, the numbers of baby boys being born are disturbingly higher than the numbers of baby girls. Invisible Girl Project, an NGO, estimates that, in India alone, between five million and seven million gender-based abortions are carried out every year.[14]

Many countries try to ban this practice, but when it is comparatively easy to determine an unborn child's gender, and when abortion on demand is available, it becomes well-nigh impossible to prevent such discrimination.

However, a similar discrimination against disabled unborn children is increasingly pursued with little or no legal hindrance. Indeed, some nations are proactively encouraging all pregnant women to have their unborn children screened for a range of disabilities, which usually results in abortion when a positive test is detected.

Abortion denies the most basic human right of all, that of life, to unborn children. Abortion on the grounds of gender or disability ensures that this denial of human rights is compounded by discrimination.

Clearly, arbitrarily limiting human rights so that they only apply after the moment of birth flies in the face of the development and progression of human rights thinking over the last few centuries. Interpreting human rights in a broader and more generous way is consistent with the worldview of reformers such as William Wilberforce, Harriet Beecher Stowe, W.T. Stead and Martin Luther King.

4

CARING FOR A CHILD WITH SPECIAL NEEDS

Pressure

It was a red-letter day when, after months of hospitalisation, Janice and I were finally allowed to take Grace home. But we discovered that the level of care Grace required was a full-time occupation. I am convinced that no-one who has not gone through the experience for themselves can ever grasp the sheer exhaustion that comes from caring for a child with special needs. We loved Grace so deeply, and her presence in our lives was a source of great joy, yet we felt that we were continually being stretched to the limits of our endurance.

The tube-feeding regime had to be maintained every four hours. We were acutely aware that, no matter how tired we might be, one mistake in the process could flood Grace's lungs with her food and cause severe illness or even death. There was a bewildering variety of medications to be applied in various forms. There were appointments with clinics, health visitors and doctors. Repeated bouts of pneumonia degraded Grace's lungs to the point where she could no longer draw sufficient oxygen from the air to breath properly. Eventually it reached the point where we had to carry huge cylinders of oxygen with us everywhere we went. The National Health Service in the UK installed a machine in our home that drew in air, enriched it with oxygen, and then piped it to outlets in different rooms of our house. Grace would wear a cannula with prongs inserted into each nostril, and then a tube ran from the cannula to the oxygen outlets. As you would expect with a young child, she was continually crawling beyond the limits imposed by her oxygen tube, suddenly being yanked back like the onrushing bulldog in Tom and Jerry cartoons that reaches the limit of its chain. Then she would get frustrated and rip the cannula out, after which we would reattach it for the umpteenth time that day. We got used to playing this game, and we gradually grew accustomed to the constant hum of medical equipment in our home – but I don't think I ever got used to the eye-wateringly high electricity bills that result from running 24-hour oxygen production in our home. We tried not to think what would happen if we ever had a fire!

We became accustomed to sleeping with part of our minds still alert for any strange sounds during the night. I vividly remember waking with a jolt one night at about 3am. I couldn't explain why, but I had a dreadful feeling that something was horribly wrong. I ran to Grace's cot and discovered that she had stopped breathing. I began to give her mouth-to-mouth resuscitation until she started breathing once more. We called an ambulance and she was rushed back into hospital. It was obvious that I had somehow wakened just as her breathing had stopped, the sudden absence of her wheezing breaths penetrating my deep sleep.

Nappy changes are part and parcel of raising any young child, but Grace's liquid diet and her medications made every bowel movement extremely messy. She had no control over her bowels and would remain in nappies for all her life. Invariably the mess

32

would seep into her clothes. We got used to the continually running washing machine and dryer.

Taking Grace anywhere was a major operation. As well as the normal paraphernalia that accompanies a young child, we also had to pack medications, a nebuliser, oxygen cylinders, a suction machine, feeding tubes, syringes, cans of liquid food, and several extra changes of clothing. We also learned essential skills such as how to tube-feed a child in the back seat of a Mini Metro!

Meanwhile, we still had to do everything that normal parents have to do. I was working two, sometimes three, jobs in order to pay the mortgage and feed the family. We still had to buy groceries, prepare food, and parent our other daughter, Kirsty, a lively and intelligent toddler who was only one year older than Grace.

During the periods when Grace was hospitalised, Janice and I would take it in turns to sit with her. Meanwhile, the rest of life continued with its demands. Sometimes the only times we would see each other would be exchanging hurried greetings as we passed each other in a hospital corridor. As a young married couple, this was not what we had envisaged on our wedding day.

I will be eternally grateful for two wonderful sources of support, without which I'm not sure how we could have ever coped – Janice's family, and the church that we belonged to at the time.

Family

Janice's sister, Fiona, moved from Northern Ireland to England to help us. Fiona suffers from a severe eye condition herself, indeed she is legally registered as blind, yet she is so resourceful and independent that you tend to forget that she's coping with such challenges. She lived in our home and helped us care for Kirsty and Grace.

Janice's parents, who also live in Northern Ireland, repeatedly travelled over to lend us help and support. They came so often that we often joked that they were single-handedly keeping the Irish Sea ferry companies in business.

At that time, we lived near Janice's grandmother, Bella McFarland, whom just about everybody called 'Granny' whether they were related to her or not! This old woman, who would survive to be 101 years old, lived for her grandchildren and great-grandchildren. Granny had not had an easy life. She and her late husband, Tommy, had followed in the footsteps of so many Irish emigrants who had moved to England and laboured hard to provide for their family. She loved Kirsty and Grace with a tenderness that was wondrous to behold. When we reached the point where we felt we couldn't cope any longer, we knew we could always visit Granny. While we went shopping or grabbed a few precious minutes snoozing on Granny's sofa, she would cradle Grace in her arms, talking to her and playing with her for hours on end.

Once again I had cause to reflect on how much we all valued Grace's life. It wasn't just the financial resources and expertise that the UK's National Health service poured into keeping her alive and treating her. So many family members were willing to cancel their plans, uproot themselves from familiar surroundings, spend a fortune on travel, simply so they could devote time and attention to this desperately sick little girl.

Not once did I ever hear a family member complain about this, or suggest that Grace's fragile life was not worth such sacrifices. Her life was seen as being just as valuable as any of the rest of our lives. Her disabilities did not lessen the value of her life, or her right to live that life, by even a fraction.

Church Community

The other great source of support for Janice and myself was the church community to which we belonged. I was serving as the assistant pastor in a Pentecostal congregation, part of the Assemblies of God denomination. Janice played keyboard in the church's worship band. We seriously wondered whether we would be able to continue with these commitments. We needn't have worried. We were about to learn just how a community looks after its own when they are facing struggles and trials.

Getting to church each Sunday was a long and complicated process. I was usually still half-asleep having driven a taxi cab the night before until the early hours of the morning. Two young children had to be fed, one normally and one via a tube-feed. Then they had to be dressed, and an assortment of medical equipment packed into bags. Then the kids had to be strapped into their car seats. This whole procedure took so long, that, by this time, Grace had often soiled her clothes and had to be dressed again. We lived less than two miles from the church, but by the time we arrived, we felt as if we had just run a marathon!

But as soon as we walked through the front doors of the church building, there was a personal reception committee waiting for us. A young woman called Judith Tiplady, a school teacher, had taken Grace to her heart in a special way. She would immediately hold out her arms, and Grace would smile and hold out her arms in return, probably relieved to be looked after by someone who seemed a bit less frazzled than her exhausted parents!

Judith was unmarried, with no children of her own, and she loved to look after Grace. She coped with everything, from nappy changes to choking fits, with infinite patience. We knew that for the two hours we were in church, unless the situation was so serious as to require an ambulance, then we didn't have to worry about Grace at all.

Meanwhile an older couple, Tom and Trisha Roberts, delighted in looking after Kirsty. Before they met each other, Tom and Tricia had both been through previous marriages, and their respective children were already grown-up. They had each done the parenting thing before, but now they had a second chance to do it together with Kirsty.

Janice and I could fulfil our commitments in church in the knowledge that both our daughters were safe and secure in the care of people who loved them. But this was not something that was programmed by a church administration. This was a community showing practical love and concern in a very natural and unforced way.

Everybody needs to belong to some kind of community. Today, many of us live in societies where we drive in and out of our properties without even discovering the names of our next-door neighbours. This need for community is so basic to our humanity that multinational corporations can earn billions by creating an imitation of it. Howard Schultz, the long-term CEO of Starbucks, is famous for saying that coffee is not Starbucks main product – they are primarily in the business of selling a community experience! Indeed, Starbucks have promoted the idea that everybody needs a 'third place' to congregate other than the home and the workplace.[15]

The 'third place' concept sounds fine in theory, but an imitation community that was dreamed up in a corporate boardroom will never be there for you when life hits a roadblock. When the doctor gives you an unwelcome diagnosis, or when your life seems to fall apart, the people who happen to share your taste for espresso-based concoctions won't be there to offer unconditional love and support!

I'm certainly not suggesting that churches are the only place where you can find this kind of community, and I've also experienced churches that had little or no sense of community at all. Yet, for us, an imperfect church full of imperfect people was where we encountered a vital network of love and support. And, whether you happen to believe in God or not, that kind of love and support is something that all of us need more of.

Being Genuinely Pro-Life

There is a famous comic strip where a crowd of people are listening to an orator proclaiming his message from a soap-box. He asks them, "How many of you think abortion is wrong?" Everyone in the crowd raises their hands. Then he asks, "So how many of you are willing to adopt an unwanted child?" This time nobody raises their hands.

On one level that comic strip implies a dishonest message. It is not fair or accurate to suggest that anyone who will not adopt an unwanted child has forfeited their right to express their viewpoint on abortion. After all, if the only people who had opposed slavery had been those who were prepared to receive a freed slave into their home, then the slaving ships would still be sailing between Africa and the Caribbean to this very day! Every one of us, with our different levels of compassion and commitment, has the right in a democratic society to speak out and express our opinion on human rights issues.

But, on another level, the comic strip highlights the need for people to be 'pro-life' in a way that goes beyond simply opposing abortion.

Judith Tiplady, and Tom and Trisha Roberts, were genuinely pro-life in that they stepped forward in a very practical way to help a young family that was struggling with a disabled child. In doing so, they also gained much joy and fulfilment – which is one reason why even the shortest and most fragile of lives is worth celebrating. Everyone's life, especially those of the weak and vulnerable, has the capacity to enrich the lives of others.

If we really believe in the value of life, then we should be affirming that by supporting and helping parents with special needs children, or by providing help to single parents and those who have experienced a traumatic or unwanted pregnancy. It isn't always easy, and can be highly emotional, but it actually adds value and meaning to our own lives.

On rare occasions, I've also encountered people who advocate capital punishment, enthusiastically support wars that result in hundreds of thousands of deaths, and want their governments to adopt immigration policies that would leave desperate refugees with nowhere to go. Yet these same people call themselves 'pro-life.' They might be anti-abortion, but they sure aren't pro-life!

Pro-Choice and Anti-Choice?

'Pro-life' is one label that is used frequently in the debate over abortion. The other is 'pro-choice.' When the debate gets particularly heated, you can also hear those who are opposed to abortion being labelled as 'anti-choice.'

On the surface, that seems like effective terminology. After all, every one of us likes to be free to exercise choices in our lives. So choice is good, right? And if someone is 'anti-choice,' then that must mean that they are evil and repressive?

Yet, when we stop to think about it, every reasonable person believes that there are some choices which should never be available to us. Nobody should have the choice whether or not they are going to enslave someone else. Nobody should be allowed a free choice whether or not to abuse a child. No civilised society thinks it's a good thing to allow others to have the choice to engage in people trafficking.

I tackled this dishonest use of language a few months ago while being interviewed by the broadcaster George Hook during his lunchtime show on Newstalk Radio. We were talking about how people get offended, or at least pretend to get offended, by the views of others. Often this faux outrage is nothing more than a smokescreen to try to blacken the reputation of someone who holds a different opinion to ours, and thereby avoid engaging in reasoned discussion with them. Then we moved on to talking about how dishonest use of language can obscure the subjects that we really should be talking about. I cited the use of the term 'pro-choice' as an example of this.

When you think about it, the debate over the Eighth Amendment, for example, is about abortion. So we have people who are pro-abortion and anti-abortion. Can you imagine if we were having that debate about something else – let's say it was about capital punishment. Now, imagine we're having a debate about capital punishment and you have pro-death penalty and anti-death penalty. And the pro-death penalty people say, 'You know what? We don't want to be called that, because we're not insisting that judges should sentence everybody to death, we simply want the judge to have a choice. So we want you to call us pro-choice.' Now, I don't think you, and other people in the media, would let them get away with that for a moment, and even more so if they began

39

saying that the people who are against the death penalty – they're anti-choice. And that's a manipulation of language.

At this point, George Hook sat bolt upright in his seat, adjusted his headset and said, "Congratulations! Thank you so much for making that point, because I hadn't thought about it at all. And I hope that didn't just make me think, but made other people listening think, because this debate is obviously going to continue until we have a referendum."

As I write this book, there is an ongoing heated national debate in Ireland over the subject of abortion. My experiences with baby Grace have convinced me that human life is of infinite value, and that every unborn child should have an equal right to be born. Birth equality, for me, is a human rights principle that will one day be as universally recognised as racial equality, the right not to be enslaved, or the right of children to be treated as human beings in their own right rather than mere property of their parents.

So you could accurately describe me as being 'anti-abortion.' I don't want to see abortion on demand introduced in Ireland, and I see selective abortion on the grounds of gender or disability to be forms of discrimination that will cause future generations to wonder how decent people could ever have tolerated such practices. I understand that in very rare medical emergencies, abortions are necessary to save a mother's life, and Irish law already allows for that. I do also understand that sometimes pregnancies can occur in heartbreakingly difficult circumstances, but I can't see how that can ever justify the taking of an innocent life. So, yes, for the same reason as I am 'anti-death penalty' and 'anti-war,' I am also 'anti-abortion.'

By the same token, those who want to see the prohibition on abortion removed from the Irish Constitution are, by any normal use of language, 'pro-abortion.' They want abortion to be legalised, they want abortion to be more freely available and, as an inevitable consequence, they want more abortions to be carried out in Ireland.

And yet many of those on the pro-abortion side of the debate, for some reason, are unwilling to be designated by the very issue that is at the core of their campaign. They are happy to use euphemisms such as 'reproductive health' or 'choice' – yet avoid using the word 'abortion' like the plague.

I find that telling. Very telling indeed.

Birth Equality

5

FACING LOSS

Time Running Out

No matter how bad a medical diagnosis might seem, you want to believe that your particular case will be the one that confounds the doctors. We were watching Grace develop an amazing little personality of her own, and we longed to be able to keep caring for her as she would experience being a teenager and a young adult. But we were aware that a large percentage of children with Familial Dysautonomia died in their infancy, and there were clear signs that Grace's lungs were continuing to deteriorate.

One of the symptoms of FD is a greatly reduced ability to feel pain. This might sound like a good thing. After all, none of us like being in pain, so surely an inability to feel pain is a good thing, right? In reality pain is our friend. Pain warns us when we are in danger of causing serious damage to ourselves and teaches us to draw back from danger. Once Grace learned how to walk, she would charge into objects, bounce off them, and fall to the ground laughing!

Thankfully Grace never broke any bones in this way, but it is not uncommon for children with FD to break arms or legs without even realising that they've hurt themselves. Grace was continually bruising herself, and her skin was so pale that sometimes the bruises looked horrific.

On one occasion, during one of Grace's frequent bouts of pneumonia, we had to rush her into a different hospital where none of the staff knew her. Remember that this was in the years before fast internet connections and the instant transfer of case files and information from one place to another.

As Grace was being admitted, Janice saw one of the nurses pull a colleague over and whisper in her ear, "We've got a child in here with unexplained bruising." If we had been with the usual nurses who knew Grace so well, they would simply have laughed with Grace and told her to be more careful. But in these strange surroundings, Janice's concern for Grace's pneumonia was compounded by an acute awareness of the nurses' whispering and accusatory stares. She endured a miserable next 24 hours until a courier delivered the files that listed the symptoms of FD and everything was explained.

It seemed so unfair. Here we were trying desperately to hold our lives together, caring for a sick little girl and trying to help her lead as normal a life as possible, pouring love and devotion into her every single day – and, for a thankfully very brief period of time, people were staring at us as if we were the kind of monsters that would harm a child.

When you are caring for a special needs child full-time, it is easy to become insulated from how other people see things. Sometimes other people avoid you, not out of any ill will, but because they don't know what to say. And sometimes you want to avoid other people, because the things that concern them so much seem a million miles away from the stuff you're living through.

As you carefully monitor your child's every symptom, you look for small improvements and little triumphs. These excite you so much that you forget that, in anyone else's eyes, your child still looks desperately sick and is getting progressively sicker.

I will never forget the one time we took Kirsty and Grace on a proper holiday. Of course we had taken them with us to stay with family in both England and Ireland, but we had never actually taken them on a real holiday – staying somewhere on our own and simply relaxing. It was something we had never been able to afford to do, but we received a small grant from the Joseph Rowntree Foundation. Joseph Rowntree was a Quaker businessman at the beginning of the twentieth century, one of the Rowntree confectioners behind such iconic brands as Jelly Tot sweets and Kit Kat chocolate bars. He devoted much of his wealth to establishing charities, including one for the benefit of families with disabled and sick children. We were able to rent a cottage for a week in the Mountains of Mourne. We had to carry all our cases on a roof-rack because the boot of the car was crammed full of oxygen cylinders and the household oxygen machine.

Of course we still had to care for Grace, and there were still tube-feeds every four hours, but by now she tolerated a semi-permanent soft-plastic feeding tube that was taped to her cheek and which ran up a nostril and then down into her stomach. She would still pull it out every couple of days, and examine it in fascination, meaning that we had to thread it back into her nose and through to the stomach again. But that was infinitely better than having to insert a hard-plastic tube down her throat for every feed with the accompanying screaming and retching. All in all, those few days in the Mourne Mountains, sitting in front of a turf fire and gazing through the windows at the beautiful scenery, were the closest thing to relaxation that we had experienced for over three years.

45

There was one interesting moment when I drove into a nearby village to pick up some groceries, and got stopped at a British army checkpoint. Remember, this was in the days when the IRA was still waging a bombing campaign in Northern Ireland. A young soldier glanced through the rear windows of my car, saw several oxygen cylinders lying on the back seat, and immediately swung his weapon round so it was trained on my face. "Sir," he called, "He's got mortar tubes in the back of the vehicle!"

I stayed very still, and kept my hands on the steering wheel where he could see them. The soldier looked impossibly young, as if he wasn't old enough to have left school, and was obviously living on the edge of his nerves. Sweat was running into his eyes, and I could see his finger tightening on the trigger. I thought to myself, "Maybe Grace is going to outlive me after all!" Thankfully, once everyone realised that I wasn't carrying any weapons, the situation calmed down and the soldiers and I all had a good laugh about it.

But it was during that same holiday that I began to realise just how disturbing others found Grace's appearance and condition.

The cottage in which we were staying was part of a little cluster of similar holiday lettings. About a hundred yards away there was a play area with a climbing frame and a sandpit. Kirsty would run down there during the day, and join in playing with other children of a similar age who were staying in the neighbouring cottages. She loved this, and we could sit on a bench outside the cottage so as to keep an eye on her.

Of course Grace wanted to go as well and join in the fun. But we were worried about her staying outside for too long. Also, Grace didn't always play well with other children. Her inability to feel pain made her absolutely fearless, and if an older child twice her size wouldn't give her the toy she wanted then Grace was very capable of charging into attack! So we tried to keep her indoors, but she kept looking out of the window and crying to be with the other children.

So, eventually we decided to take her to the play area. We wrapped her up in a jacket, scarf and gloves – even though it wasn't that cold a day – and Janice walked hand-in-hand with her. I followed behind carrying an oxygen cylinder.

As soon as we reached the other children, they stopped what they were doing and stared open-mouthed at Grace. One of the younger girls nervously hid behind her big sister. Suddenly I began to realise what Grace must look like to them. Our obviously sick daughter, with a plastic cannula carrying oxygen into her nose, a large yellow tube taped to her cheek and running up a nostril, and a gas bottle following her wherever she went.

In no time at all, the parents of the other children came out to see what was happening. Janice explained to them about Grace, and they made all the correctly sympathetic comments. Then, in a very polite way, they made excuses about why their children had to go back to their own cottages. Soon we were standing alone in the play area with Kirsty and Grace.

I think that was the first time that I began to really try to see Grace as others saw her. We were getting excited over slight and temporary improvements, but everyone else looked at her and saw just how sick she was. I began to appreciate that, unless something pretty miraculous was going to happen, we should treasure every moment we had with Grace as if the days were diamonds and the minutes were gold dust.

For the rest of that holiday we still enjoyed ourselves, but when the other children were playing in the play area, we would let Kirsty join them, but kept Grace with us as we watched. But any time we noticed that the play area was empty, we would take both Kirsty and Grace there and let them play happily together.

Moments to Treasure

A few weeks after that holiday, Janice returned from the shops and announced that the local pharmacy was running a 'Bonniest Baby' photo competition. You could pay to get a portrait photograph of your child, and the kid that was judged to be the prettiest would win a cash prize. "Let's take Kirsty and Grace there," she said, "You never know, they might win a prize."

Now, Kirsty was the cutest-looking little girl imaginable, and to this day I think that the competition must have been fixed, otherwise she would definitely have won the cash prize! But, I thought to myself, there was no way in the world anyone could ever describe Grace as a bonny baby!

I looked at Janice, but I couldn't work out how to say what I wanted to say. We loved Grace with all our hearts, her physical challenges were part of the person we loved, and to us she was truly beautiful – but I knew that the kind of people who judge 'Bonniest Baby' competitions were working off a different set of criteria. Most other people couldn't see the beautiful Grace that we knew, all they could see was a sick child.

And then I looked at Janice, and realised that this woman I had married had far more sense than I would ever possess. She didn't care what any competition judges thought about Grace's appearance. We were going to have a special day out with both of our daughters, and we were going to pay a photographer to capture the moment.

So we dressed the girls up and took them in for their photographs. The photographer was extremely professional, and if he was shocked by Grace's appearance he certainly didn't allow it to show. Afterwards, everyone agreed that Kirsty's photograph really looked tremendous. As I've already said, the competition must have been a fix for her not to win first prize!

As for Grace, her photograph sits in front of me now as I write this chapter. She is dressed up in her best clothes, and we'd temporarily removed the cannula and the feeding tube. Grace hated sitting still for any length of time, so instead of looking directly at the camera, her gaze is looking over the photographer's shoulder where Janice was performing some kind of mime to keep her attention. You can tell that all is not as it should be with this child. Her hair is sparse, there are rings round her eyes, and one cheek has slight yellowish bruising where the tape holding her tube in place had been attached. Her face is somewhat puffy, due to the steroids that she had been taking to combat her lung deterioration, and her mouth betrays the high and narrow arched palate that is characteristic of Familial Dysautonomia.

Grace's photograph didn't win any prizes either, of course, but it *is* beautiful. And every time I look at it I feel a mixture of loss and gratitude. I mourn the absence of Grace, even after so many years, and I'm saddened when I think of all the aspects of life that she never lived long enough to enjoy. But I also feel profoundly thankful that she enriched our lives for the time that she did. And I'm thankful to have a wife with the good sense to enter our children into that competition and ensure we kept a record of a priceless memory.

There are other memories of Grace that will remain with us for ever. She loved to sing, even though the problems with her palate meant that most people who didn't know her well enough couldn't actually distinguish the words coming out of her mouth. Even her regular caregivers had to struggle to interpret her words at times. When she was in hospital, the nurses on the children's wards would teach her nursery rhymes and such, but more than anything else Grace wanted to sing the songs she heard in church each week. One afternoon I arrived at the hospital to find Grace in her cot, surrounded by half a dozen nurses. Grace was singing a worship song from church, with her hands lifted in the air just like any happy-clappy Pentecostal. The nurses, none of whom were in the slightest bit religious, also had their hands in the air and were singing the words that Grace had taught them!

Grace loved watching short Disney cartoons. We had a few video tapes that we replayed so often that I'm amazed they didn't actually wear out. She would roar with laughter every time at the same places, usually when Donald Duck or Goofy fell flat on their faces.

She also got engrossed in watching other people playing video games. Grace's own hand-eye coordination meant that she just got frustrated trying to handle the controls herself. But she was happy to watch others playing, and used to point her finger and cackle uproariously every time Sonic the Hedgehog lost another life!

We began to realise that when Grace reached school age, assuming that she would live that long, she wasn't going to be able to attend a mainstream school. So we began looking at brochures for various special schools.

Kirsty attended a small school that was run by our local church. Each morning, as her older sister left for school in her blue and red uniform, Grace would watch her wistfully. Under normal circumstances we, as parents, would have been encouraging her, telling her that next year she would be going to school like that. But we all knew that wasn't going to happen.

Yet, on one memorable occasion, Grace did get the opportunity to wear that coveted uniform. Kirsty's school was participating in a musical concert one evening at church. Lynn Barton, a teacher at the school, worked to ensure that Grace could stand with them. She managed to produce a tiny version of the school's uniform for Grace to wear, making a skirt and going to the extent of knitting a tiny jumper for her and stitching the school badge onto it. It brings tears to my eyes to think how many hours she must have poured into that act of kindness to a pupil's sister.

That evening, as the schoolchildren filed up on to the stage to sing their song, Grace joined them in her little uniform and stood beside her sister on the stage. She didn't even try to sing any of the words of the song, but stared out across the audience with a huge grin on her face. None of us knew that it would turn out to be the one and only time in Grace's life that she would get to don a school uniform. It was a very special moment for her and also for us.

I don't know what it cost, in time or money, to kit Grace out in that uniform for the few minutes that the schoolchildren were up on that stage. Whatever it cost, the look on my daughter's face that night was such that I would have gladly paid a thousand times as much for such a precious moment and a priceless memory.

Celebrating the Gift of Life

One of the most important things that Grace taught me was to enjoy every precious and precarious moment of her life. With a severely ill or disabled child, there will always be the tendency to dwell on the brevity of their lifespan, or what they couldn't do, or what didn't happen. But we don't do that with other people. We don't view someone's life as wasted if they die at the age of 55 when others live to be 100. Nor do we say that our loved ones' lives were not worth living because they didn't do something as outwardly significant as Bill Gates or Nelson Mandela.

This is why society has radically changed the way it marks the deaths of stillborn children. At one time, such babies were privately and unofficially buried in unconsecrated ground, or even tossed into a ditch like a piece of rubbish. To their shame, churches were largely responsible for this by their insistence that the stillborn child, by reason of not being baptised, did not qualify for participation in religious rites or ceremonies.

In Ireland, it was not unknown for priests to conduct an 'conditional baptism,' using phrases such as "if thou art a man" (if the baby was misshapen enough not to look human)[16] or "if thou art alive,"[17] thus permitting the child to be buried in a church cemetery. But often grieving parents were left to bury their babies near pre-Christian centres of belief, such as fairy trees and fairy forts, or even on the other side of a cemetery boundary wall, as close to church property as possible.

It is ironic to consider that, for most of Irish history, the general population was much more convinced of the personhood of the unborn child than the church was. And yet today it has become fashionable to decry any concern for the welfare of unborn children as an intolerable imposition of Catholic dogma upon the rest of us.

Until comparatively recently, mothers in hospitals were not permitted to hold their stillborn child, the birth was not registered or certified, and parents were not told how their dead child was disposed of. Gradually, realising that this was causing mental torment, cemeteries began cordoning off separate sections for stillbirths – often known as 'little angels' plots. However, these were, in truth, usually nothing more than mass graves.

Thankfully attitudes have changed, both unofficially and in government policy. Today, most hospitals give parents an opportunity to grieve, hold their child, take photographs, and to commemorate the death of their stillborn baby in a way that marks the end of a life, rather than treating them as an anticipated life that never actually happened. Nurses will often dress the stillborn baby in nappies, even though the child will never have the opportunity to soil the nappy, because they realise there is a great psychological need in most mothers to mark the fact that they parented a baby through months of pregnancy.

Since 1995, it is a legal requirement that all stillbirths occurring in Ireland must be registered at the office of the Registrar of Births, Marriages and Deaths. There is also a provision for parents to retrospectively register stillbirths that occurred before 1995 – a wise and compassionate ruling that gives some sense of closure to parents who felt that previous legislation treated their babies as if they had never existed.

Under the present legislation, stillborn children must be given a first name and a surname, and they are allocated a PPS number – just like every other person in Ireland. Parents are also entitled to maternity and paternity leave and benefits, exactly as if their child had been born alive. Ireland is not unique in this, nor is this in any way influenced by religious dogma. In fact, the move to legally recognise the personhood of stillborn children who never lived outside the womb is predominantly occurring among secular western nations, rather than in more religious societies.

Such moves are obviously welcome to most parents of stillborn babies. In many countries, parents are also campaigning for the age at which a baby's death is classified as a stillbirth rather than a miscarriage to be lowered (in Ireland, in order for a child's death to qualify as a stillbirth, the baby must weigh at least 500 grammes or have a gestational age of at least 24 weeks). Parents who lost children at an earlier stage of development often feel strongly that their babies also are worthy of legal recognition.

Most of us would have great sympathy for those parents, and would instinctively support their campaign to have their babies legally recognised as having existed. Somewhat surprisingly, their efforts are sometimes opposed by those who claim to be defending women's rights! For example, in Australia, the Women's Abortion Action Campaign opposes such a step as "a slippery slope."[18] This is because abortion on demand, for a great many people, can only be sustained by denying that the unborn child is a human being.

This means, for abortion advocates (and particularly for those who seek the legalisation of late abortions), that there is an ideological need to promote a definition of personhood that begins at birth - from the moment that a child emerges from the womb. Irish law, and compassionate common sense, recognises that the stillborn baby was a person – even meriting a name and a PPS number. If that is the case, then it is an inescapable fact that to abort an unborn child of a similar gestational age constitutes the killing of a person. There is a mutual contradiction here. You cannot logically or coherently support compassionate legislation for parents bereaved of stillborn children and yet simultaneously support abortion on demand.

This ideologically-driven push to deny personhood and humanity to an unborn child takes us into the very heart of the abortion debate. Despite the attempts of some to portray it as such, this is not a conflict between religion and secularism. The issue of how we define personhood and humanity, and how our ideology can cause us to deny others the status of human beings, is at the core of some of the world's greatest abuses of human rights.

How do we decide who is a human being, and who is not? Should such definitions be determined by common sense, by science, or by our own ideologies or dogma? What are our motivations in defining personhood? Should we be as broad and as generous as possible in defining a human being, seeking thereby to ensure that we don't infringe on the human rights of others, or is it permissible to hold to a narrow and restrictive definition of humanity so that we can avoid stopping practices that we very much want to continue?

6

THE DEHUMANISATION AGENDA

The Limits of Science

So how are we to decide who does or does not qualify as a human being? Can science help us answer this question?

This is not necessarily the same as asking when life begins. Science tells us that life begins at fertilisation, when the sperm and the egg combine to form a unique genetic entity. This is why it is plainly unscientific to claim, as Noam Chomsky did in a speech at University College Dublin in 2013, that an unborn baby is simply part of a woman's body.[19] The unborn baby has a distinct DNA that differentiates it from the mother's bodily parts which all carry her own DNA. Medical textbooks agree that fertilisation marks the *beginning* of a separate human being's development, but scientists disagree as to when the child becomes a human being in its own right.

Some scientists do indeed see fertilisation as the beginning of personhood. Others point to implantation (at about 7 days), to gastrulation – the point at which twinning is no longer possible (day 14), to the first heart beat (day 18), to the point at which an embryo becomes a foetus with all structures in place in a rudimentary form (week 8), to 'quickening' when the movements of the unborn child begin to be felt (week 14), to the point at which the unborn child can possibly survive as a premature baby (week

21 or 22), to the point when a distinct pattern of brainwaves can be detected (24 weeks), or to the moment of birth.

There is, then, no scientific consensus as to when an unborn child becomes a person, or a human being in its own right. Surveys reveal that scientists are hopelessly divided on the issue. For example, a poll of doctors and medical students in a large English hospital revealed that just over a third thought human life begins at conception, just under a third thought it happened at birth, and just over a third thought human life begins at some other point in the womb.

To make things more complicated, the answers of those doctors and medical students were shaped in some measure by their religious beliefs. Of those who professed some religious belief, half believed that human life begins at fertilisation. Among those with no religious belief whatsoever, the most common opinion was that human life begins at some point after fertilisation, but before the point of birth.[20]

Dogma & Ideology

For many religious people, their faith informs them as to when personhood begins. Many Catholics, for example, accept the pronouncement of their church that life begins at conception. Similarly, many Protestants reach the same conclusion based on their understanding of the Bible.

Those people who are not religious object, very understandably, that religious dogma is no basis on which to frame legislation in a secular democracy. Laws passed on the basis of religious dogma have, throughout history, sometimes been the source of great cruelty. 'Because my church (or my holy book) says so' is not going to persuade those who don't happen to share your faith.

We need to recognise, however, that non-religious ideology has just as much capacity to cause harm when it is forced on other people. The greatest atrocities of the twentieth century were not caused by religious zealots, but by people pursuing political ideologies that either treated religion as an irrelevant distraction, or actively suppressed it.

The insistence among pro-abortion advocates that a baby does not become a human being until the point of birth is every bit as much a dogmatic statement as the religious insistence that personhood commences at fertilisation. It is not based on any scientific consensus and goes against the experience and instinct of most parents.

At this point we need to be aware of something called 'confirmation bias.' This is a psychological phenomenon that all of us can fall into at one time or another. Confirmation bias causes people to interpret information in a way that will support and validate their existing beliefs.

The early Enlightenment thinkers fell into the snare of confirmation bias when they denied the full humanity of African people. They believed in the rights of man, but they also profited from slavery and colonialism. If they acknowledged Africans as human beings with the same rights as white Europeans then, in order to be consistent with their beliefs in the rights of man, they would have to make personal sacrifices. Instead, they chose to interpret the differences in lifestyle and appearance of Africans as evidence that they were not fully human and were incapable of being civilised.

We see a similar process among the most zealous pro-abortion advocates who insist that abortion should be available up to the point of birth. Their ideological commitment to abortion is often part of a wider worldview. Yet presumably they would be horrified at the thought of killing infants (even though the practice of late abortion results in numbers of babies who survive the process either being killed by lethal injection *after* birth, or being left untended to die). Therefore, in order to maintain their commitment to making late abortions available, these activists *must* define personhood as not beginning until the child emerges from the womb.

This is a classic case of confirmation bias, defining a human being in a way that suits your own agenda. Indeed, when we look at the history of human rights abuses, this redefinition of what it means to be human is a common tactic.

Dehumanising

When people want to take away someone else's human rights, the first step is to stop treating them as human. This is why advocates of slavery, rejecting the abolitionists' portrayal of the African as a man and a brother, tried to portray blacks as less than human.[21]

Regimes that practice torture know that it is important to make their victims seem less than human. This removes the inhibitions that might otherwise stop the torturers from inflicting the required levels of suffering.[22] For example, camp guards under Cambodia's Khmer Rouge regime were viewed as being insufficiently brutal in their treatment of prisoners. This was addressed by reducing the living conditions to such levels of degradation that the guards

60

would view the prisoners as filthy animals rather than human beings.[23]

This dehumanisation tactic was employed to great effect by the Nazis. Propaganda posters and cartoons routinely portrayed Jews as vermin and insects. A popular children's book, *Der Giftpilz* (The Poisonous Mushroom), compared Jews to poisonous mushrooms that had to be rooted out and eradicated.[24] If children could be taught to think of Jews in such non-human terms, then recruiting them to participate in the Holocaust would become easy.

Leading up to the Rwandan genocide in 1994, a Hutu radio station, Radio Télévision Libre des Mille Collines, broadcast a non-stop stream of propaganda that repeatedly referred to the Tutsi tribe as 'cockroaches.'[25] After all, once you begin to view people as being insects then it becomes easier to stamp on them. Lest we pride ourselves on being too civilised in the West to fall into such a trap, consider how those opposing immigration have also used dehumanising language to compare migrants to a swarm of insects.[26]

We see a similar process in action when abortion advocates refuse to speak about an 'unborn child,' preferring to refer to 'the foetus,' or even to 'a clump of cells.'[27] Indeed, some have taken this dehumanising of the unborn child even further, adopting a Kantian definition of humanity and arguing that since an unborn child cannot make choices, it is, by definition, not human. By extension, this argument can be used to deny the true humanity of new-born infants also.[28]

One huge problem with ideologically-based definitions of personhood, particularly ones that would narrow or limit those whom we recognise as human beings, is that they tend to be motivated by a desire to maintain a practice that would become indefensible once we acknowledge that other human beings are being adversely affected by it.

A prime example involves the fight to abolish slavery. When Wilberforce and others campaigned against slavery, they had no selfish interest in doing so. They did not stand to profit in any shape or form if slavery was abolished. In fact, there was a widely-accepted argument that the British Empire could not prosper without slavery, and that economic recession would follow abolition.[29]

For those who wanted slavery to continue, of course, there was a clear selfish motive. The pro-slavery advocates wanted their profits to continue. Recognising black Africans as human beings would threaten those profits. Therefore, despite not having the slightest scientific support for doing so, they denied that Africans were fully human.

We need to ask hard and searching questions of those who would assert, without any evidence, that human personhood does not begin until the point of birth. Parents choose to have abortions for all sorts of reasons, of course. Sometimes there are heart-breaking circumstances involved. But we must also acknowledge that many abortions are carried out for less dramatic reasons.

The Guttmacher Institute, an American pro-abortion group, surveyed over 1200 women in 2004 to discover why they had an abortion. Here are the top ten contributory reasons (the respondents were free to identify more than one reason):

Having a baby would dramatically change my life – 74%
Can't afford a baby now – 73%
Don't want to be a single mother or having relationship problems – 48%
Unmarried – 42%

Would interfere with education – 38%

Would interfere with job / employment / career – 38%

Have completed my childbearing – 38%

Student or planning to study – 34%

Have other children or dependents – 32%

Not ready for a(nother) child – 32%[30]

All of these are major life-impacting scenarios. I don't think any of us would see any of the above reasons as being trivial. But, crucially, neither do I think that any reasonable person would see any of these as justifiable reasons to end the life of another human being.

Therefore, for advocates of an abortion on demand regime such as operates in the United States, there is an ideological imperative to define 'human being' in a way that excludes the unborn children who will be affected by abortions for all the reasons listed above. And we should be very suspicious of any attempt to limit and narrow the application of human rights based on an ideological assertion, without scientific evidence, and where self-interest inevitably plays a major role.

Common Sense

There is an old saying, often attributed to Mark Twain, that says "The problem with common sense is that it's not that common." Nevertheless, common human experience can often help us reach wise and humane conclusions.

For example, in order for slavery to be abolished, it wasn't enough for the abolitionists to quote the Bible – even though most of them were deeply religious. They had to demonstrate that their campaign was in tune with ideas of justice and fairness shared by most normal people. The science of genetics had not developed to the point where it could prove that blacks of African descent were just as fully human as white Europeans. But Harriet Beecher Stowe's novel, *Uncle Tom's Cabin*, achieved what was, at that point in time, impossible for science. By describing the experiences and feelings of those suffering under slavery, she helped those who had previously been sitting on the side-lines to articulate what, deep down, they already knew to be true – that people were human beings irrespective of the colour of their skin.

When someone insists that an unborn child does not become a human being until the moment of birth, it is reasonable to ask why they have, without any scientific evidence, chosen this arbitrary point for recognising personhood. Usually, when pushed for an answer, they will base their reasoning on one of four arbitrary characteristics: size, level of development, environment and degree of dependency (these can be easily remembered by using the acronym SLED).

Is it reasonable to deny the status of a human person on the basis of size? It is certainly true, as pro-abortion advocates like to point out, that unborn children are smaller than other human beings – indeed, in the early stages of a pregnancy they are tiny. But why should this be used as a measure of humanity? A three - year-old child is much smaller than a thirteen-year old, but we do not therefore conclude that the three year-old is less of a person. Indeed, we usually recognise the vulnerability of smaller people by giving them more legal protection.

It makes no more sense to use level of development as a basis for determining humanity. A toddler is less developed than an adult. For example, a five-year-old girl can't bear children because her reproductive system is as yet undeveloped. But we wouldn't dream of saying that her lack of development makes her less of a person than a young woman.

But what about environment? Should it make a difference that the unborn child lives in a sac surrounded by amniotic fluid rather than breathing air like the rest of us? Hardly. Changing your environment does not change your status as a person. If you were to take up scuba diving, and spend some of your time underwater and breathing compressed air from a tank on your back, that would not make you more or less of a human being. It is equally ridiculous to believe that the brief journey down the birth canal into a different environment suddenly transforms a non-person into a person.

As for degree of dependency, this is one of the sillier arguments against recognising an unborn child as a human being. The fictional television doctor, Gregory House, famously broke the news to a young woman that she was pregnant by saying she had 'a parasite' and then adding, "Don't worry. Many women learn to embrace this parasite. They name it, dress it up in tiny clothes, arrange playdates with other parasites."[31] Unfortunately, this portrayal of the unborn child is not confined to fictional TV. I have encountered it in serious debate. For example, consider the following quotation:

> *Most foetuses are in the mother's womb because the mother consents for this situation, but the fetus is there by the mother's freely granted consent. But should the mother decide that she does not want the fetus there any longer, then the fetus becomes a parasitic "invader" of her person, and the mother has the perfect right to expel this invader from her domain.*[32]

A parasite, as Dr House would have known if he were a real doctor, is an organism that lives on, and draws nutrition from, a host of another species.

But an unborn child certainly is dependent and, at least in the earlier stages of a pregnancy, is unable to survive if removed from the mother's uterus. Does this level of dependency mean that it is not a human being?

You might as well argue that a conjoined twin is not a human being, or that a person with a profound physical or mental disability is less than human. If someone is in a coma following an accident, even temporarily, does their level of dependency stop them from being human?

Sometimes, even those who are most committed to denying the humanity of the unborn child forget themselves and, lapsing into ordinary humane language, refer to the unborn child in terms that convey personhood.

For example, I was driving my car while listening to a radio interview with a particular politician who has been very vocal in advocating abortion on demand. This politician has repeatedly used dehumanising language such as 'a clump of cells' when referring to unborn children.

On this occasion she was describing a heartrending case where an expectant mother had discovered that her baby had a severe abnormality and had travelled to the UK for an abortion. She finished by saying, "And this poor mother had to bring her baby home in a cardboard box!"

At that point I nearly swerved off the motorway. I looked at my car radio and said, "Oh, so now it's a baby!"

A few days later, I mentioned this in an online debate with a pro-abortion advocate. Her response was, "Yes, if it's wanted, then it's a baby. If it's not, then it's a foetus."

The problem with this view is that it destroys the entire basis of human rights. The very reason why so many people are denied basic human rights is because they are unwanted by others. If we make 'being wanted' the basis on which we determine whether someone is a human being or not, then human rights legislation becomes meaningless.

Irish Minister for Social Protection, Leo Varadkar, even though he sees Ireland's abortion laws as too restrictive when a woman's health is likely to be affected by pregnancy, has spoken out against the use of dehumanising language. A qualified medical doctor himself, Minister Varadkar said that it would be 'offensive' to ask a pregnant friend how her 'foetus' was doing.

> *I met a friend of mine for dinner on Saturday night and she was pregnant, expecting her first child . . . I did ask her if she knew what sex the baby was. I didn't ask what sex the foetus was.*
> *If I did ask her about her foetus, she would have been quite offended.*
> *And the same goes for my sisters because, to me, a foetus is a medical word. It's like talking of your glossus instead of your tongue or your digits instead of your fingers.*
> *I often wonder why people use that word.*
> *It is yet to be explained to me why people use a medical word to talk about what is a form of human life, if not a person.*[33]

During the Citizens' Assembly, designed to discuss the issue of abortion and present recommendations to the Irish government on abortion, testimonies were heard from people on both sides of the debate.

One testimony was from a lady who was told by her doctors, at 12 weeks pregnant, that her unborn child would not survive until birth. She travelled to England for an abortion, rather than just waiting in the knowledge that the baby would die anyway.

Having lived through our experiences with Grace, I can only imagine the distress this woman was going through. But what struck me about her testimony of her ordeal was that she repeatedly referred to the unborn child as her 'baby' – using the language of personhood. She also mentioned that they subsequently held a service for the dead child after her return to Ireland.[34]

I found it significant that her testimony, at least as it was reported in the press, implicitly acknowledged that she was carrying a fatally ill baby.

The situations of parents caring for terminally ill children, both before and after birth, is obviously highly emotional and needs to be approached with great sensitivity. But in the midst of it all we should always remember that we are talking about a human being.

Trusting Women

In 2016 the British Pregnancy Advice Service (a bit of a misnomer since the BPAS is a major abortion provider) launched a campaign to remove all legal restrictions whatsoever against abortion in the UK – seeking for it to be legal to abort a child right up to the moment of birth for any reason whatsoever.[35] Their campaign used the slogan 'We Trust Women' (with the obvious implication that anyone who doesn't subscribe to their agenda doesn't trust women).

In one sense this is a powerful slogan. Women have historically been discriminated against, disenfranchised and disempowered. Indeed, abortion continues to discriminate against women as it is more often used to abort girls than boys.

The problem with this slogan is that nobody would ever dream of using such a poor argument in any other area of life. If you take any group of people as a whole, you might trust them in general, but that does not exempt them from laws that are designed to protect the vulnerable.

I trust mothers to care for their toddlers. The vast majority of women care for their infant children in ways that are selfless and, at times, quite heroic. Yet we still have laws that make it illegal for parents to leave their children unattended in a car on a hot summer's day. Should we campaign for the repeal of such laws on the basis that we aren't trusting mothers? Are such laws caused by mother-hating old men? Of course not! We trust parents in general, but we still enact compassionate laws to protect young children from the tiny minority of parents who betray that trust.

Similarly, most husbands care for their wives. As a church minister I conduct weddings, and I trust each bridegroom to treat his bride with honour and respect. But I still support laws that make it illegal for a man to rape his wife. Why? Because trust extended to husbands as a general group does not remove society's responsibility to protect women from husbands who are brutes and bullies.

And so it is with pregnancy. We trust pregnant mothers to care for their unborn child – and the great majority of them do. They take every precaution to protect the little life they are carrying, and encourage their husbands or partners to lay their hands on their bump to feel the baby kicking (quite convinced that what is kicking is a little person, and not a 'clump of cells'). Many pregnant mothers talk and sing to their unborn child, and most abstain from intoxicants that might harm the child.

But we would be foolish in the extreme if we were to assume that such trust means that every pregnant mother will do what is best for their child. Not even the most ardent pro-abortion advocate would truly believe such a claim. Just walk for a few hours in the centre of any Irish town or city and you will see positive proof that a small minority of pregnant mothers will quite deliberately choose to act in ways that are detrimental to the well-being of their child – as evidenced by smoking while obviously pregnant.

In other words, extending trust to a group as a whole does not preclude recognising that a small minority within any group of human beings will act in ways that harm and abuse the weak and the defenceless. And supporting legal protection for the vulnerable does not make us anti-women, or betray any lack of trust.

The 'We Trust Women' slogan is a dishonest and illogical attempt to marginalise and silence those who have a genuine desire to protect the human rights of the vulnerable. It is also used hypocritically to imply that half the population of Ireland have no right to express an opinion on this issue because they happen to be male and 'only women should decide' (while simultaneously embracing pro-abortion groups that are led by men and receiving financing from male billionaires).

If Ireland is going to face a referendum on abortion, then Ireland deserves a reasoned debate about abortion. That debate should be open to everyone who cares about human rights. Such a debate is not well-served by untruthful soundbites.

In fact, while we are discussing trusting women, it is worth noting that opinion polls show marginally more women than men favour keeping Ireland's prohibition against abortion.[36] In the UK, the gender difference is more pronounced with polls consistently showing many more women than men are in favour of restricting abortion.[37]

There is a very good reason for this, and it comes back to common sense. No man has experienced what it is like to carry another life inside us. Many of us have tried our best to empathise, but sitting beside your wife or partner and feeling her bump kicking falls a long way short of the mother-child bond that develops during pregnancy. Those who have experienced pregnancy and motherhood are in a better position than anyone to share their view of whether they were carrying a bunch of cells or a human being. Most mothers that I have spoken to are firmly convinced that they were carrying a person inside them.

This is why hospitals dress up stillborn babies to pose for photographs with their bereaved parents. This is why our government insists that babies who never lived until birth are still granted a name and a PPS number. This is why Leo Varadkar sees it as offensive to ask a pregnant friend how her 'foetus' is doing. This is why the anonymous lady who testified to the Citizens' Assembly spoke so movingly about her 'baby.' This is why Janice and I were every bit as emotionally involved in Grace's battle for life before birth as we were after birth. Because the natural instinct of parents, and especially mothers, recognises that the unborn child is a person who is worthy of recognition as such.

Safety First

In the absence of any scientific consensus as to when someone becomes a human being or person, and recognising that religious and ideological dogma do not provide an agreed basis for legislation, it seems reasonable to take into account the common view that personhood occurs at some point before birth.

It would be fair to say that many, if not most, people see a child's status as a human being beginning at some point in the womb. That is why many countries that do permit abortion on demand do so only in the early stages of pregnancy. In most

European countries, for example, abortions after 12 weeks are limited to certain conditions. The United Kingdom has one of the higher limits for abortion on demand at 24 weeks, which is also the limit established by the Supreme Court of the United States in its Roe versus Wade case, under which women are constitutionally entitled to an abortion.

The fact that such limits exist at all, and the way they vary from country to country, is evidence that legislators are unsure at what point personhood begins, and are nervous about allowing abortion during the later stages of pregnancy.

One serious problem with late abortions is that they spill over into the killing of children *after* birth. In one year alone, according to a report by the Confidential Enquiry into Maternal and Child Health, commissioned by the UK Government, 66 babies that survived abortion were left to die.

Guidance from the Royal College of Obstetricians and Gynaecologists recommends babies over 22 weeks which survive abortion should have their hearts stopped by lethal injection but this can be a difficult procedure for doctors.[38]

By anyone's definition, those 66 babies were living, breathing human beings. To kill them by lethal injection, or to leave them untended to die, was murder, and an undeniable violation of their basic human right to life.

I would suggest that, if law-makers are not sure when personhood begins, then they have a responsibility to adopt an approach which minimises possible harm. For example, when countries pass laws forbidding drink-driving, they don't set the permissible blood-alcohol limit at the point where the average person becomes intoxicated. They choose a much lower limit, reasoning that the potential harm caused by preventing a sober driver from going on the road is much less than the potential harm caused by erring in the other direction, and permitting a drunk driver to kill someone. And, as most of us know, the safest policy is not to drink and drive at all.

In the same way, we should balance the potential harm of preventing abortions if personhood had not actually begun, against the potential harm of killing unborn children who are indeed human beings. Applying this reasoning, one does not need to be religious or dogmatic to see the wisdom of being cautious and avoiding aborting unborn children.

Birth Equality

7

A SHORT BUT SIGNIFICANT LIFE

Returning Home

We had been living in the Northwest of England, but now we moved back to Ireland so that I could concentrate on starting a new church congregation in Drogheda, County Louth. Even though it meant a long commute for me, we had to live in Northern Ireland rather than in the Republic. Our medical team in England could easily send files to Belfast and communicate with doctors there who also worked for the UK's National Health Service, but they felt that dealing with another nation's health system could easily result in delays or misunderstandings that might prove fatal to Grace.

There was also much doubt whether the government in the Republic would actually be prepared to subsidise the massive costs of Grace's medical treatment in the same way that the UK was doing. Not only that, as far as anyone was aware, no doctor in the Irish Republic had any experience whatsoever in treating FD. Also, Janice's parents lived in Belfast and we wanted them to be able to spend more time with Grace. All things considered, it was better that we lived north of the border.

Grace's lung function continued to worsen. At one point the hospital doctors believed that they could prolong Grace's life by inserting a gastrostomy tube directly into the stomach, bypassing the oesophagus and thereby preventing food from being aspirated into the lungs. They also wanted to perform a fundoplication procedure, where the entrance to the stomach is surgically tightened to avoid reflux back into the oesophagus.

Janice and I were reluctant to go ahead with this, worried about whether Grace, who often tore her feeding tube and nasal cannula out in a temper tantrum, might do the same with the gastrostomy tube. Also, Grace had managed to stay out of hospital more recently, and we hated the idea of her enduring major surgery followed by a long period of hospitalisation. Nevertheless, we agreed to the surgery, being assured that the risks were low and that the possibility of a longer lifespan would be worth it all.

However, on Grace's next visit to hospital, the anaesthetist who would be sedating Grace for this operation confided to Janice that he was really worried about it. He explained that Grace's unique condition created added complications, and that there was a significant risk that she would die during the operation or that she would suffer brain damage.

Janice and I sat down and talked for a long time about our hopes and fears for our youngest daughter. In the end we made one of the hardest decisions of our lives. We decided that the risk of Grace dying on the operating table, combined with the prolonged hospitalisation that would follow and the impairment of her quality of life from the gastrostomy tube, were too high a price to pay when there was no guarantee that her life would be significantly lengthened as a result. We withdrew our consent for the operation, judging that quality of life was more important than quantity of life, and we determined to enjoy to the fullest every day that we had with our daughter.

As it turned out, we were to have almost a full year more with Grace. We rented an old house on the seafront in Bangor, County Down, and we became a familiar sight in that area as we walked along the beach with our daughters, our dog, and a bottle of oxygen!

We made the most of every day. Never more so than on 13th of June 1994. The next day was our wedding anniversary, but I was due to drive down to Portlaoise and Cork for a three-day trip to visit some churches, so we decided to celebrate as a family the day before the anniversary. It was a beautiful Summer day, so we took the girls to the nearby town of Donaghadee and found a sandy beach. As Grace paddled alongside Kirsty in the sea, managing to be surprised every time a wave came in as if she had never seen it happen before, I hugged Janice and said, "I'm so glad that we made the decision to let her live her life to the full." We talked about holding a joint birthday party in August (Kirsty would be six on 17th of August, I would be thirty-two on 19th of August, and Grace would be five on 20th of August).

That night, as I gave Grace her final tube feed before she went to bed, she choked some of the food back up and began coughing and spluttering. That was hardly an unusual event, so I cleaned her up and lay her down to sleep.

In the morning, Grace's wheezing seemed to be a little worse, so we gave her some medication via a nebuliser machine. As I left for Portlaoise, Janice said, "I know it's no worse than usual, but if she keeps wheezing like that I'll take her in and get her checked over."

That evening, as I was finishing up in Portlaoise, I got a phone call to say that Grace had taken a turn for the worse and that Janice was taking her to hospital in Belfast. I wasn't unduly alarmed, after all, we'd been through this same scenario dozens of times. I phoned the church in Cork, told them I couldn't make it the next day because my daughter was sick, and drove straight back to Belfast. This was before mobile phones were widely available, so I had no more communications on the journey.

When I arrived at the Royal Hospital for Sick Children in Belfast, I made my way, as usual to the ward where they always treated Grace. As I entered the ward, a nurse stopped me and asked me where I was going. I said, "I'm here to see Grace Park – she's back visiting you all again!"

The nurse looked at me strangely and replied, "Just wait here and I'll get someone to see you." I was ushered into a side room. Then a doctor came and explained that they had done everything they could to save Grace's life, but that the strain on her heart had been too much and it just gave up. I sat and stared at the floor tiles, unable to take in what I was hearing. Then Janice came into the room and we collapsed in tears in each other's arms. It was our eighth wedding anniversary.

Shock and Grief

The following few days, including Grace's funeral, all seemed to pass in a blur. We took Kirsty and stayed with Janice's parents between Grace's death and the funeral. I remember a sleepless night, and then being woken in the afternoon to take a phone call of condolences from someone who I knew quite well, and for the life of me I couldn't recognise his name and wondered who he was. The day before Grace's funeral I felt as if I had to get out of the house, so I visited someone else I knew slightly. After sitting chatting with them for a few minutes, I realised that they hadn't heard about Grace's death. Absurdly, I didn't want to upset them by sharing bad news, so I sat and drank tea and chatted with them as if everything was normal for another hour before returning to Janice's parents.

Once again we discovered the importance of belonging to a church community. A couple from church realised that we would be unable to face up to clearing out Grace's room, so they took the key to our house and bagged up all her clothes and medical paraphernalia.

We discovered in those first few weeks of mourning just how much of a toll nearly five years of dispensing medication and carrying out tube feeds had taken. I slept like never before. It had been so long since we had been able to sleep a whole night through without getting up for a tube feed, to change a nappy, or simply to check Grace was breathing OK.

Sometimes I would wake up and just enjoy the sensation of being able to rest. Then the memories would come flooding back and I would remember with horror that the only reason I was able to rest was because of my daughter's death. Then I would be overwhelmed with guilt for enjoying resting.

The reason I share this, difficult and personal as it is, is because I occasionally hear people saying that it would be better for disabled children if they were never born at all. This can easily become the rationale for aborting a disabled child, on the basis that it is kinder for them. Some take this reasoning further. In 2014 the biologist, Richard Dawkins, claimed that it would be immoral to allow a baby with Down's Syndrome to be born.[39]

Grace taught me that a human life, even a short one lived with a condition such as Familial Dysautonomia, is something precious to be appreciated. Ending her life before birth would not have been kinder for her in any way. It would certainly have made life easier for us as her parents, for caring for a disabled child can be incredibly hard work, but it would be very wrong indeed to rationalise such a decision to pretend it is being done for the child's sake rather than for the parents' sake.

Janice grieved long and hard for Grace. That was probably wise. I suppressed my grief, throwing myself more and more into my work. The new church in Drogheda continued to grow, and we moved across the border to County Louth in 1995. After Grace's death, there was no longer any reason to remain in Northern Ireland. I worked harder and harder, but overwork doesn't deal with grief and pain – it only stores it up for later. Things came to a head in 1997.

I was invited to Ukraine to teach at a conference for church leaders. I agreed, not realising at the time that it would involve me flying out on our wedding anniversary. Of course, to make matters worse, this would also be the third anniversary of Grace's death. Sometimes I demonstrate such little sense that it is a source of amazement to me that Janice still loves me and remains married to me!

I was feeling guilty at travelling when my place was probably at home with my wife, and was trying not to think too much about it being the anniversary of Grace's death. I decided to distract myself by concentrating on the inflight video.

Austrian Airlines had obviously decided, given the mix of nationalities on this flight, that it would make more sense to show videos that had no dialogue, therefore there would be no need for translation. The first presentation was a Mr. Bean comedy. Then they began to show short Donald Duck movies. I realised that these were the same movies that Grace had loved so much.

To my horror, all the grief I had been suppressing for three years began to come to the surface. I could feel tears coming to my eyes. "Oh no!" I thought, "Please don't let me start crying in public while watching a Donald Duck cartoon!" Too late! Now the tears were flowing freely, and soon I was trying to stifle huge audible sobs. The man sitting beside me leaned over and whispered in my ear, "Don't worry. It's not real – it's only a cartoon!"

After that embarrassing incident I had to face up to my grief, and to stop suppressing the painful memories. I embraced the pain and the sense of loss, but also remembered with gratitude so many meaningful moments spent with Grace.

The pain of losing a child dulls with time, but it never completely leaves you. Twenty-three years later Grace still visits me in my dreams, and sometimes a snatch of music, something on television, or a smell from the kitchen triggers a meaningful memory.

Birth Equality

I have briefly shared with others our experiences with Grace over the years, particularly when my role as a church leader involves helping other people through times of grief and loss. But I never intended to write about it in this depth or to be so open about the emotional impact of her life and death.

But the current debate about abortion and the Irish Constitution touched a nerve with me. Frequently I heard pro-abortion advocates talking about children with disabilities as if their lives were somehow less valuable. I realised that Ireland was in danger of copying other countries that allow abortion to be used as a discriminatory tool to abort unborn children with conditions much less severe than Familial Dysautonomia.

Most of all, I was provoked into action by a dishonest tactic that is being employed by many of those who are pushing for the Irish Constitution to be changed so as to allow abortion on demand. I realised that they were using the comparatively tiny number of ethically difficult cases, involving rape victims or unborn children with severe disabilities or abnormalities, and trying to make the narrative all about these 'difficult cases' in order to push an alternative agenda – to usher in an abortion regime similar to those in other European countries where perfectly healthy unborn children, or those with conditions entirely compatible with enjoying life, such as Down's Syndrome, are denied the right to be born.

Writing about Grace has been a very emotional experience. Her short life touched so many other people in so many ways. Janice and I have learned to treasure the time we spent with her, just as we treasure our relationship with our other wonderful daughter, Kirsty. Grace taught me that all human life is precious and valuable. She helped me realise that every child deserves the opportunity to be born, and that for a society to affirm birth equality as a human rights principle is something to be celebrated.

8

ABORTION & HUMAN RIGHTS

No Human Right to Abortion

The Universal Declaration of Human Rights, adopted by the United Nations General Assembly in 1948, is seen as the most important definition of human rights. It was framed as a response to the horrors of Nazism, the Holocaust and the Second World War. It was a rejection of the principle that 'might is right' – recognising that nations have a duty to care for their citizens and that there should be limitations to a State's power over its citizens.

So, according to the Universal Declaration, which rights do we class as human rights? Which rights are so fundamental that to deny them is to deny our very humanity?

The first, and most fundamental, right is the right to life. Without this, quite obviously, all other rights become meaningless. Other fundamental rights include freedom from slavery, freedom from torture, freedom of speech, freedom of religion, freedom of movement and the right to a fair trial.

The right to life, freedom from torture and freedom from slavery are, in international law, considered to be *jus cogens* norms. They are non-derogable, meaning that there is no circumstance, including national emergency or warfare, where there is any conceivable excuse for these rights to be violated.[40]

Subsequently, the United Nations has developed seven core treaties which make the freedoms in the Universal Declaration binding on all nations which sign up to them. These treaties are:

1. The International Covenant on Civil and Political Rights
2. The International Covenant on Economic, Social and Cultural Rights
3. The Convention on the Elimination of All Forms of Racial Discrimination
4. The Convention on the Elimination of all Forms of Discrimination Against Women
5. The United Nations Convention Against Torture
6. The Convention on the Rights of the Child
7. The International Convention on the Protection of the Rights of All Migrant Workers and Members of their Families

These seven treaties, known as the human rights instruments, provide the basis for human rights law. When nations sign up to these treaties they agree to be bound by international law. This means the human rights in the treaties supersede national laws.

Abortion is a controversial area of human rights. None of the major international treaties or core human rights instruments list a right to an abortion, and the European Court of Human Rights does not recognise an entitlement to abortion.[41] In the words of Baroness Nuala O'Loan, human rights lawyer and Northern Ireland's first police ombudsman, "There is no human right to abortion."[42]

But there is a human right to life. Indeed, it is the basic human right without which all others become meaningless. International treaties are worded in ways that will guarantee the maximum buy-in from nations, for, without widespread ratification, a treaty is toothless. It should not surprise us then, that the major human rights treaties carefully avoid defining when personhood begins.

The United Nations did not want to alienate countries that permit abortion, nor those that restrict abortion.

Article 1 of *The Convention on the Rights of the Child* says this:

For the purposes of the present Convention, a child means every human being below the age of eighteen years unless under the law applicable to the child, majority is attained earlier.[43]

The key question, then, is whether we class an unborn child as a human being.

When do Human Rights Begin?

So, do the major human rights treaties give any guidance to help us decide when personhood begins, or what constitutes a human being? Surprisingly enough, they do.

The Preamble to *The Convention on the Rights of the Child* reads as follows:

Bearing in mind that, as indicated in the Declaration of the Rights of the Child, "the child, by reason of his physical and mental immaturity, needs special safeguards and care, including appropriate legal protection, before as well as after birth"[44]

'Before, as well as after birth.' Advocates for abortion claim that since this wording is in the Preamble, rather than any of the Articles of the Convention, it can be ignored. But that is to fundamentally misunderstand the purpose of a Preamble to a treaty or constitution.

A Preamble is not an enforceable part of a treaty, and cannot overrule anything stated elsewhere in a treaty, but it is legally significant in that it exists to help interpret the rest of a treaty, particularly when there is any ambiguity. Indeed, the European Court of Human Rights has ruled that the Preamble of a convention should, as a matter of good faith, be referred to and taken into account when interpreting the Articles of that same convention.[45]

Furthermore, Article 24 of *The Convention on the Rights of the Child* states specifically that signatories to the convention have a duty "to ensure appropriate pre-natal and post-natal health care for mothers."[46] Pre-natal care, in a treaty dealing with children's rights, by definition refers to caring for a human being that has not yet been born.

To sum up, then, *The Convention on the Rights of the Child* was deliberately ambiguous in its definitions so as to ensure that countries which practise abortion would not face sanctions – such countries would otherwise have refused to ratify the convention. But a natural reading of the convention in good faith clearly indicates that the unborn child has human rights and is entitled to protection.

This understanding of the Preamble and the rights of the unborn child was reinforced in the Irish High Court in July 2016, when a judge ruled that the government must consider the human rights of an asylum-seeker's unborn child before issuing a deportation order. Justice Richard Humphreys quoted *The Convention on the Rights of the Child* in his judgement.[47]

It makes perfect sense, therefore, for anyone with a genuine passion for human rights, to feel a deep concern about the protection of the unborn child.

Most of us, religious or not, feel very uneasy when we see an obviously pregnant woman smoking. This is not because we think that damage might be caused in the future when the child will become a human being. No, we instinctively sense that harm is being caused now to a human being who deserves better.

The Eighth Amendment

Ireland, since 1983, has an amendment to its Constitution providing protection to the unborn. This states:

> *The State acknowledges the right to life of the unborn and, with due regard to the equal right to life of the mother, guarantees in its laws to respect, and, as far as practicable, by its laws to defend and vindicate that right.*[48]

In effect, this means that abortions may not be carried out in Ireland unless the mother's life is in danger. The Eighth Amendment, which passed in a referendum by 66% to 33%, took abortion legislation out of the hands of politicians and placed it in the hands of the people, as the Constitution can only be changed by another referendum. This is fitting, as human rights should not be subject to the whim of politicians. That is particularly apt in a context such as Ireland's, where a political party rarely gains a working majority in elections, and governments are formed through backroom deals with independent politicians and special interest groups.

There is presently a well-funded and highly-organised campaign to see the Eighth Amendment repealed. Pressure from overseas is being brought to bear on Ireland, and companies that run abortion clinics in other nations are also attempting to influence Ireland so as to see a market open up here.[49]

Opinion polls indicate that over 80% of Irish people would be opposed to the introduction of abortion on demand, but a majority would favour abortion being available in extreme cases such as where the mother has been raped or the baby is suffering from an abnormality that is so severe as to be incompatible with life.[50] The danger, of course, is that such extreme cases only constitute a tiny percentage of abortions carried out in most western countries. Therefore, there is a very real fear that the compassion people feel for those in extreme circumstances will result in a removal of Constitutional protection for *all* unborn children – paving the way for abortion on demand to be introduced in opposition to the will of the people. A recent opinion poll indicates that many Irish voters are aware of this danger, with more supporting reform of the Eighth Amendment than outright repeal. Interestingly, the same poll indicates that a majority of Irish voters think that, when it comes to any of the ten reasons most commonly given for obtaining abortions in the United States[51], abortion should not be permitted in Ireland[52]

Certainly there is a need for Ireland to work out how to compassionately respond to some of the very difficult ethical dilemmas caused by the very small number of 'hard cases' when it comes to our abortion laws. But a kneejerk reaction that opens the door to abortion on demand would be a human rights catastrophe.

We also need to remember that you do not promote one person's human rights by removing someone else's basic right to life. As I discovered with our daughter, even a short life lived with limitations and disabilities can be precious and significant.

The dilemma of women who are pregnant through rape is another thorny issue. Such women have already had one of their most basic human rights violated in a most horrendous way. But the damage caused by that human rights violation will not be removed by a further human rights violation against the unborn child. In Ireland, we do not sentence rapists to death. It seems strange, therefore, that we should advocate death for unborn children because their fathers were rapists.

There has also been confusion due to statements from United Nations bodies condemning Ireland's ban on abortion as violating human rights, even though there is no such thing as a human right to an abortion. These statements are often misreported in the Irish media with headlines such as "UN says Ireland's abortion ban cruel, inhuman or degrading!"[53]

Anyone reading such headlines might imagine that Ireland had violated one of the major international treaties, or that the United Nations General Assembly passed a resolution condemning Ireland. That, of course, is not the case. The United Nations has a number of committees, councils and commissions which offer non-binding and often highly-politicised opinions. Being criticised by one of these bodies does not equate to 'the United Nations' condemning anyone.

Indeed, certain United Nations bodies have a long history of expressing partisan political opinions. In 2003 Colonel Gaddafi's Libya was selected to chair the UN Human Rights Commission.[54] For years the UN Human Rights Council issued numerous condemnations of Israel while failing to condemn North Korea or Zimbabwe, and refused to censure the Sudanese government for its campaign of genocide and systematic slavery in Darfur. Members of the Council in 2006 included such human rights champions as Algeria, China, Cuba, Pakistan, Russia and Saudi Arabia.[55]

Those who are genuinely interested in human rights should be more concerned about protecting vulnerable human beings than in the pronouncements of ideological and political partisans.

I strongly believe, not due to religious dogma, but because of a concern to protect the most vulnerable in society, that Ireland's Eighth Amendment is a valuable human rights protection. A few years ago, the children's charity, Barnardos, suggested Constitutional changes to protect the rights of children in Ireland. In a document in which they quoted the text of *The Convention on the Rights of the Child* (including the Preamble), they argued that their proposed changes were appropriate given that "it is not unusual for the State to acknowledge specific situations where people are unique and vulnerable, (for example, the unborn)".[56] I agree with Barnardos' assessment of the State's responsibilities. Unborn children are people. They are unique and vulnerable. Therefore it is indeed appropriate to defend their human rights in the Constitution.

The campaign for repeal likes to pretend that Ireland is backward and needs to be dragged into the 21st century. I would contend that the opposite is the case. The Eighth Amendment represents a forward-thinking approach to human rights which will one day be adopted by other nations.

Notes

[1] McKenna, Jarrod. "Religion and Politics is Like Ice-Cream and Manure: They Don't Mix." *Sydney Morning Herald*. 6 September 2013

[2] Baldry, H.C. *The Unity of Mankind in Greek Thought*. Cambridge: Cambridge University Press, 1965. 97

[3] Locke, John. *The Second Treatise on Civil Government*. New York: Walter J. Black, 1947. 78

[4] Bernasconi, Robert & Mann, Anika Maaza. "The Contradictions of Racism" in Andrew Vallis (ed.) *Race and Racism in Modern Philosophy*. Ithaca,NY: Cornell University Press, 2005. 92

[5] Cohen, William B. *The French Encounter with Africans: White Response to Blacks, 1530-1880*. Bloomington,IN: Indiana University Press, 1980. 88

[6] Wheeler, Roxann. *The Complexion of Race: Categories of Difference in Eighteenth-Century British Culture*. Philadelphia,PA: University of Philadelphia Press, 2000. 186

[7] Billington, Ray. Living Philosophy: *An Introduction to Moral Thought (Third Edition)*. London: Routledge, 2003. 101

[8] Bernasconi, Robert. "Kant's Third Thoughts on Race" in Stuart Elden & Eduardo Mendieta (eds.) *Reading Kant's Geography*. Albany,NY: State University of New York Press, 2011. 301

[9] Veyne, Paul. *The Roman Empire*. Cambridge,MA: Belknap Press, 1987. 9

[10] Levittan, Michael. "The History of Infanticide: Exposure, Sacrifice, and Femicide." In Angela Browne-Miller (ed.) *Violence and Abuse in Society: Understanding a Global Crisis. Volume 1: Fundamentals, Effects, and Extremes*. Santa Barbara,CA: Praeger, 2012. 123

[11] Lebra, Joyce. "Women in Service Industries." in Joyce Lebra, Joy Paulson & Elizabeth Powers (eds.) *Women in Changing Japan*. Stanford,CA: Stanford University Press, 1976. 107

[12] Soderlund, Gretchen. *Sex Trafficking, Scandal, and the Transformation of Journalism, 1885-1917*. Chicago: University of Chicago Press, 2013. 24

[13] Engs, Ruth Clifford. *The Progressive Era's Health Reform Movement: A Historical Dictionary*. Westport,CT: Praeger, 2003. 4

[14] Huizhong, Wu. "Activists Go Undercover to Expose India's Illegal Sex-Selective Abortions." *www.cnn.com* 27 March 2017

[15] Ferrell, O.C. & Hartline, Michael D. *Marketing Strategy: Text and Cases (Sixth Edition)*. Mason,OH: South-Western, 2014. 2

[16] Hurd, William. *A New Universal History of the Religious Rites, Ceremonies, and Customs of the Whole World*. Blackburn: J. Hemingway, 1799. 272

[17] Barry, J.J. "Medico-Christian Embryology" *St. Louis Medical and Surgical Journal. 4,6.* 1867

[18] Kennedy, Duncan. "Should Stillborn Babies be Given Birth Certificates?" *www.bbc.com* 14 May 2012

[19] Gleeson, Colin. "Chomsky Criticises Restrictive Abortion Laws." *Irish Times.* 3 April 2013

[20] Kearney, Dermot. "The Beginning of Life: UK Report – a Survey Among Doctors & Medical Students." *Catholic Medical Quarterly. Volume 67 (1).* February 2017

[21] Chelst, Kenneth. *Exodus and Emancipation: Biblical and African-American Slavery.* Jerusalem: Urim, 2009. 64

[22] Haritos-Fatouros, Mika. *The Psychological Origins of Institutionalized Torture.* London: Routledge, 2003. 176

[23] Hinton, Alexander Laban. *Why Did They Kill?: Cambodia in the Shadow of Genocide.* Berkeley,CA: University of California Press, 2005. 237

[24] Pine, Lisa. *Education in Nazi Germany.* Oxford: Berg, 2010. 58

[25] Ilibagiza, Immaculée. *Led by Faith: Rising from the ashes of the Rwandan Holocaust.* Carlsbad,CA: Hay House, 2008. 5

[26] Elgot, Jessica & Taylor, Matthew. "Calais Crisis: Cameron Condemned for 'Dehumanising' Description of Migrants." *The Guardian.* 30 July 2015

[27] Macagno, Fabrizio & Walton, Douglas. *Emotive Language in Argumentation.* New York: Cambridge University Press, 2014. 3

[28] Fagot-Largault, Anne. "The Notion of the Potential Human Being" in David R. Bromham, Maureen E. Dalton & Jennifer C. Jackson (eds.) *Philosophical Ethics in Reproductive Medicine.* Manchester: Manchester University Press, 1990. 151

[29] Howley, Frank. *Slavers, Traders and Privateers: Liverpool, the African Trade and Revolution, 1773-1808.* Birkenhead: Countyvise, 2008. 215

[30] Finer, Lawrence B; Frohwirth, Lori F; Dauphinee, Lindsay A; Singh, Susheela & Moore, Ann M. "Reasons U.S. Women Have Abortions: Quantitative and Qualitative Perspectives." in *Perspectives on Sexual and Reproductive Health 37,3.* September 2005. 113

[31] "Maternity" *House.* Season 1, Episode 4, 43 minutes. First broadcast by Fox, 7 December 2004.

[32] Rothbard, Murray N. *The Ethics of Liberty.* New York: New York University Press, 2002. 98

[33] O'Keefe, Alan. "Don't Use Foetus When You Mean Baby: Varadkar." *Irish Independent.* 22 November 2016

[34] Duffy, Rónán. "My Only Thought was if this Plane Crashes Everyone is Going to Know that I'm Pregnant." *www.thejournal.ie* 4 March 2017

[35] Petre, Jonathan & Adams, Stephen. "End the Time Limit for Abortions, Says Midwives Chief." *The Mail on Sunday*. 15 May 2016

[36] "Irish Times/Ipsos MRBI Poll" *www.irishtimes.com* 12 October 2016

[37] Robbins, Martin. "Why are Women More Opposed to Abortion?" *The Guardian*. 30 April 2014

[38] Marsh, Beezy. "66 Babies in a Year Left to Die after NHS Abortions That Go Wrong." *The Daily Mail*. 4 February 2008

[39] Bingham, John. "Richard Dawkins: 'Immoral' to Allow Down's Syndrome Babies to be Born." *The Telegraph*. 20 August 2014

[40] Pati, Roza. *Due Process and International Terrorism: An International Legal Analysis*. Leiden: Koninklijke Brill, 2009. 260

[41] Londono, Patricia. "Redrafting Abortion Rights Under the Convention: A, B and C v. Ireland." in Eva Brems (ed.) *Diversity and European Human Rights: Rewriting Judgments of the ECHR*. Cambridge: Cambridge University Press, 2013. 95

[42] Connolly, Marie-Louise. "Abortion: 'Ridiculous' that NI Operates Under 1861 Termination Law, Says Lord David Steel." *www.bbc.com* 22 April 2016

[43] Detrick, Sharon. *The United Nations Convention on the Rights of the Child: A Guide to the "Travaux Préparatoires."* Dordrecht: Martinus Nijhoff, 1992. 119

[44] Detrick, Sharon. Op.cit. 100

[45] Sinclair, Ian. *The Vienna Convention on the Law of Treaties (Second Edition)*. Manchester: Manchester University Press, 1984. 128

[46] Grover, Sonja C. *Children Defending their Human Rights Under the CRC Communications Procedure*. Heidelberg: Springer, 2015. 128

[47] Binchy, William. "Constitutional Rights of Children Apply to the Born and Unborn." *Irish Times*. 18 August 2016

[48] Moriarty, Bríd & Massa, Eva. *Human Rights Law (Fourth Edition)*. Oxford: Oxford University Press, 2012. 48

[49] Ryan, Órla. "British Group Launches Helpline for Women in Ireland Who Buy Abortion Pills Online." *www.thejournal.ie* 1 September 2016

[50] "Irish Times/Ipsos MRBI Poll" *www.irishtimes.com* 12 October 2016

[51] Finer et al, op. cit., 113

[52] Leahy, Pat. "Poll Shows Public Support for Abortion is Cautious and Conditional." *Irish Times*. 3 March 2017

[53] Edwards, Elaine. "UN Says Ireland's Abortion Ban Cruel, Inhuman or Degrading." *Irish Times*. 9 June 2016

[54] Slann, Martin. "The United Nations and Democratization" in Jeffrey Haynes (ed.) *Routledge Handbook of Democratization*. Abingdon: Routledge, 2012. 307

[55] Mertus, Julie A. *The United Nations and Human Rights: A Guide for a New Era (Second Edition)*. Abingdon: Routledge, 2009. 45

[56] *Information Pack. Children's Rights*. Dublin: Barnardos Training & Resource Service, 2008. 13